"*Anarchic Agreements* is a kind something not often codified, mu comprehensive care—forming effe of groups, consistent with anarchist aspirations and insights. It addresses the nitty gritty of working well together, a focus that everyone who wants a better world ought to prioritize".
—Michael Albert, economist, political analyst, and author whose recent books include *No Bosses* (2021) and *Practical Utopias: Strategies for a Desirable Society* (2017)

"I've been using the tools and principles in the *Anarchic Agreements* pamphlets since 2017—here they are at last as one book, with more besides. The book works with campaign groups, charities, housing co-ops, workers' co-ops, and all sorts of organisations and committees that aspire to be less hierarchical or to work better with volunteers. Making agreements that are consensual, changeable, and conscious is the keystone for making groups that last. It can also be a tonic for groups that have gone stale, inherited old rules, or need a new shared vocabulary to move from a vision of the future to the real thing".
—Jed Picksley, community organiser, trainer, activist, and permaculturist

"Informed and informative, this is a rare and much-needed response to the often-simplistic approaches to anarchist organising. For every piece of practical advice useful to organisers, there's an equally valuable reflection on the complexities of working together without hierarchies. I couldn't recommend this more highly for newcomers to horizontal organising—and I'd make the case that it should be mandatory reading for anarchist veterans!"
—Matthew Wilson, author of *Rules without Rulers* (2014)

Anarchic Agreements

A Field Guide to Building Groups and Coalitions

Ruth Kinna, Alex Prichard, Thomas Swann, and Seeds for Change

Anarchic Agreements: A Field Guide to Building Groups and Coalitions
© Ruth Kinna, Alex Prichard, Thomas Swann, and Seeds for Change
This edition © 2023 PM Press.

ISBN: 978–1–62963–963–5 (paperback)
ISBN: 978–1–62963–978–9 (ebook)
Library of Congress Control Number: 2022931960

Cover by John Yates / www.stealworks.com
Interior design by briandesign

10 9 8 7 6 5 4 3 2 1

PM Press
PO Box 23912
Oakland, CA 94623
www.pmpress.org
Printed in the USA

Contents

Preface to the
PM Press Edition

An anarchist constitution might sound like a contradiction in terms. Our aim is to convince you that it's not. This short book shows how to constitutionalise in an anarchistic way, explaining the theory and giving examples from anarchist and anarchistic groups. It is one of the products of over ten years of academic research, but it is designed explicitly for practical everyday purposes, not academic ones. What we do in this very short book is show you some of the ways you can do it, in plain simple English, with practical examples and illustrations dotted throughout, and with some past and current constitutions for you to look at for inspiration at the end. The focus is not what's in these documents. It is instead on the ongoing and never-ending process of developing constitutions and keeping those documents alive, in the fairest and least-dominating ways possible. If you want to find out more about the research project see www.anarchyrules.info. If not, just read on.

Why is anarchist constitutionalising never ending? Because power in society is always changing, and how we understand oppression changes and evolves. Power could be economic—a minority might have more money than others and, together, oppress the majority (consciously or unconsciously). Or some people might have a monopoly on information and use that intellectual power to exclude others. Or some people might benefit from the legacy of racism and colonialism, or heteronormativity, or just because they're men. Constitutions are one tool in the battle against domination and oppression.

We constitute ourselves when we collaborate with others: constitutionalising is just a way of deciding how we want to do this. At a bare minimum, how we constitute ourselves challenges, divides and balances power, and because there is never a point at which our social relationships can be harmonised perfectly, once and for all, we must keep on reviewing how we do this.

Constitutions are designed and built as pacts or agreements that can progressively equalise power relations, create standards for the relationships between one group and another, and specify when and under what conditions these standards can be challenged, revised, or even disposed of all together. Because society is always changing, as is our understanding of it, so should our constitutions.

Constitutionalising is a package of activities that we generally think of separately, but which all work to challenge, divide, and balance power. So constitutionalising is not only about writing documents and poetic preambles (the declarations that often come at the start of a constitution) that call a people into being (like "we the people" and so on). Constitutionalising also involves setting out the rules of a community, as well as dividing power into institutions and sub-groups, and specifying how these groups relate to one another. It is also about developing decision-making procedures, such as majoritarian democracy or consensus decision-making.

Constitutions not only solidify the culture of a group and give it political power; constitutions also curb the arbitrary (unconstitutional) decision-making power of hidden groups, e.g., cliques or friendship groups, and they do this by making those groups visible, balancing them against other groups, and establishing transparent decision-making processes. Rules, institutions, decision-making processes and the poetic preambles, work together in complex and highly dynamic ways to prevent one person or group of people—a king or a parliament or a council—from arbitrarily dominating others.

Our guidance on constitutionalising should not imply that anarchists have ever been enthusiastic defenders of the existing constitutions of states and nations. Not at all. Voltairine de Cleyre, for example, summarised her objection to constitutionalism in her 1893 essay, "In Defence of Emma Goldman". Here she wrote that "the constitutional right of free speech", which Goldman had been accused of flouting, "is a meaningless phrase". She rejected constitutions because they neither write nor enforce themselves. Her views are worth quoting at length:

> [T]he constitution of the United States, and the Declaration of Independence, and particularly the latter, were, in their day, progressive expressions of progressive ideals. But they are, throughout, characterized by the metaphysical philosophy which dominated the thought of the last century. They speak of "inherent rights", "inalienable rights", "natural rights", etc: They declare that men are equal because of a supposed, mysterious wetness, existing somehow apart from matter. I do not say this to disparage those grand men who dared to put themselves against the authorities of the monarchy, and to conceive a better ideal of society, one which they certainly thought would secure equal rights to men; because I realize fully that no one can live very far in advance of the time-spirit, and I am positive in my own mind that, unless some cataclysm destroys the human race before the end of the twentieth century the experience of the next hundred years will explode many of our own theories. But the experience of this age has proven that metaphysical quantities do not exist apart from materials, and hence humanity cannot be made equal by declarations on paper. Unless the material conditions for equality exist, it is worse than mockery to pronounce men equal. And unless

> there is equality (and by equality I mean equal chances
> for everyone to make the most of himself), unless, I say,
> these equal chances exist, freedom, either of thought,
> speech, or action, is equally a mockery.

De Cleyre's arguments are more or less the common sense of the radical left now. She believed that our ideas about what is right and wrong change and that the balances of social power do, too. No constitution can predict and anticipate these, nor can constitutions easily accommodate them. All constitutions will eventually buckle and break unless they are grounded in and reflect a progressive material equality, where people have sufficient amounts of what they need to live fulfilling lives. The problem with government constitutions, backed by authority, is it that they remain fixed when conceptions of equality and equity and distributions of material power change. The lesson of de Cleyre's argument is to understand rule-making—constitutionalising—as a never-ending process: one that demands that you pay attention to the individuals and groups who get to make rules and accrue power and to the democratic mandates you need to challenge these tendencies.

The examples at the back of this book and those on our website (see www.anarchyrules.info) show that radical constitutionalising works. Our view is that it provides a dynamic model for social change and that constitutional reform on the standard model in modern nation states is a poor alternative.

Iceland gives us one of the rare examples of what could be called a "crowd-sourced" constitution, one which was radical in terms of its participatory design, if not its content, but which has yet to make a lasting impression. In the wake of the catastrophic financial crisis of 2008, a constitutional council was elected to develop a new constitution. Over the next five months, the panel invited the public to participate in the process. This involved a large group of non-experts discussing their ideas online and gathering public opinion on what should and should not go into the new constitution. When the document was drafted, they took that new constitution to parliament for discussion before possible ratification. In 2012, the constitution received public support through a national referendum, but, in 2013, it stalled in parliament and has, at the time of writing, still not been ratified. The reform efforts failed, and the old constitution is still in place.

Anarchists should find real value in the Icelandic experience, because it shows it's possible to engage large groups of people in constitution-writing processes. At the same time, the Icelandic experience reinforces anarchist arguments about the barriers to transforming existing institutions from within. In the context of nation states and capitalism, the idea of constitutional change is utopian. In simple terms, modern state constitutions reflect the interests of the most powerful individuals and groups in society, and changing those constitutions would mean changing their interests, which is unlikely if that involves taking away their power and privilege.

For anarchists, a genuinely crowd-sourced constitution, built from the bottom up, doesn't enshrine the power of wealthy and politically influential groups, and it requires revolutionary processes, not just reform. What revolution involves is another debate, but if people are not empowered to make their own rules, constitutions will always fail them. Unless power is taken away from established groups such as the political class or wealthy capitalists, then no constitution will truly enable self-government.

If the parliamentary path to this sort of radical change is closed, then maybe a path that goes around parliament is needed. For anarchists, the alternative is to "build the new in the shell of the old", to quote from the preamble to the constitution of the Industrial Workers of the World (see "Appendix One: Declarations"). Constitutionalising then takes place on the streets, and in our homes, workplaces and communities.

The constitutional process we discuss here should not be confused with democracy, nor is democracy or the will of the people always antithetical to the constitution of a society. The argument of this book is that constitutionalising—the process of balancing power relationships—requires more than simply organising decision-making differently. It is not enough to just deliberate in radically democratic ways, such as through consensus. Anarchist organisations and the forms of constitutionalising—of constituting themselves as groups and communities—they put into practice are not immune to the flaws that Voltairine de Cleyre identified in the American constitution. They are equally subject to what Robert Michels dubbed the "iron law of oligarchy", the tendency of all organisations, no matter how democratic, to concentrate power in fewer hands over time. What is special about anarchists, as Michels observed, is that they are acutely aware of this tendency and are proactive in devising fluid constitutional solutions to counter it. The iron law of oligarchy demands a corresponding drive to anarchist constitutionalising, and this is much more complex than articulating the "people's will".

In anarchist constitutionalising, power is constrained and enabled by the conscious and changeable, consensual interactions of the groups and individuals who participate in associations. Those associations can link up on the same basis. We do not advocate the "scaling up" of anarchist experiments, where they get bigger and bigger over time, because of the tendency towards oligarchy in such large organisations. Rather, we argue that groups, like individuals, should constitutionalise.

Part one of this short book explains how groups can form and constitutionalise in an anarchist way, and part two looks at how these groups might form coalitions, without sacrificing more autonomy than is absolutely necessary for the pursuance of common goals. All coalitions should be temporary, and like all groups, the exit option, or secession, is sacrosanct.

In the appendices, we include some historic and contemporary examples of anarchist and anarchistic constitutions, rule books and reflections, to illustrate the breadth of scope of writings on this topic, and to inspire you to get thinking and acting.

Ruth Kinna, Alex Prichard, and Thomas Swann
2022

Acknowledgments

The original Anarchic Agreements pamphlets that form the basis of this book were written with Seeds for Change, an activist training and research organisation, and circulated in the UK as printed pamphlets and online between 2018 and 2021. We are grateful to Seeds for Change for their participation and for helping to give our academic ideas wider appeal. Thanks also to Jed Picksley for sharing her experiences of using the original pamphlets to help reconstitute a whole range of UK-based organisations. The worksheets at the back of this book were designed and written with her help and constructive input. We are also grateful to members of the Wales, Ireland, England and Scotland Regional Administration of the Industrial Workers of the World (IWW) and Radical Routes for allowing us to work with them and for their permission to reprint a selection of their formal documents in appendix one. Thanks also to Hartford Cohousing for permission to reprint their documents. We reached out to the other groups included but did not receive a reply before we went to press. We are also grateful to all the groups that shared with us how valuable they found the initial pamphlets, from social enterprises in Copenhagen to autonomous spaces in Iceland and housing co-ops in Bristol. This project was made possible by funding from the UK Economic and Social Research Council (ESRC) and Loughborough University. All author royalties from the sale of this book will go to Seeds for Change.

How to Build Durable Groups

Introduction

> "According to the constitution..." "That's against the rules..." "Our media policy bans us from..." "The correct procedure is..."

For many people, the language of constitutions, policies and procedures is associated with having to play by someone else's rules. Social and environmental justice groups often resist the many powers in the world that are telling us what to do, so creating new rules may feel like the last thing we want to spend time on. Can rules and constitutions play a role in creating groups that are liberating and empowering to be part of?

This guide looks at the questions that need to be answered when we transform from a series of unconnected individuals into a collective that can use the words *we* and *us* to describe itself. These questions might include: What is the purpose of the group and what are its core values? How are decisions made? How do different tasks get done in the group? What rules and policies does the group need? How can the group empower its members, as individuals and as a collective?

We call the process of answering these questions *constitutionalising*. This isn't necessarily about creating a written constitution. It could simply mean working out a shared understanding about who the group is and how it goes about doing things. The decisions a group makes about these questions make a big difference to the experience of the people involved and to what the group can achieve. In some ways, the process the group goes through to make those decisions is even more critical. This first part looks at how we can make constitutionalising an empowering process for groups. Part two looks at the ways in which empowered groups can constitutionalise wider coalitions in equally anarchic ways.

Key Principles

Broadly speaking, the agreements a group makes will be more empowering for the people involved if they are *consensual*, *changeable* and *conscious*.

Consensual

Often, we associate rules with being told what to do by people who have authority over us—from the adults who raised us, to the teachers at school, the line managers in workplaces, the officers in benefits agencies, landlords, social norms, elected officials in the local council and government... Many of us get very little chance to have a say in the rules that dictate what we can and can't do.

On the flip side, a complete free-for-all also leaves many of us with very little control over what happens to us. If our housemate smoking inside affects our asthma, most of us would think it was alright to ask them to go outside. Some people would pre-empt the issue by talking about it before they move in—along with other issues like bills, cleaning and shared food.

Consensual agreements are created by the people who are affected by an issue. To be genuinely consensual, everyone should be able to shape the agreement, or at the very least have their needs taken into account. It isn't always easy to find a solution that works for everyone, even on a simple question like what day of the week to have a meeting. But if everyone is part of shaping the agreement, the answers we reach are more likely to be fair.

The main pitfall of trying to be consensual is that it can take a lot of time. The energy it takes to create inclusive decisions on every question affecting how the group works may make it hard to do anything else. Protracted meetings about policies could lead to the group losing the people who are most keen to get things done. This can also exclude the people whose time is most limited, whether because of health, caring commitments, work or simply because they have a lot of other things going on in their lives. Many groups need to prioritise carefully to ensure that important decisions get everyone's consent without the whole group getting so bogged down that it grinds to a halt.

Changeable

If a group sets up agreements or rules that everyone consents to, there is still a need to revise those agreements over time. If new people join, established members alter their views, or circumstances change, the agreements may need to change too to reflect that.

Groups will need to find a balance between the benefits of a stable group and the benefits of a group reflecting the views of all its members. Usually, new people are invited to join based on a clear agreement about what the group is for and what values it holds. This helps create stability, by limiting the changes a group needs to consider. An anti-nuclear power group wouldn't be expected to become pro-nuclear because someone joined the group and said they didn't agree with what it was all about.

Even if a group doesn't change its fundamental principles lightly, it can be flexible about how those principles are achieved. For example, a group which is committed to non-hierarchical organising might think very carefully indeed before introducing a system of elected leaders. However, it could experiment with different *methods* for reaching decisions with the input of the whole group. In other circumstances, a group may need to make more fundamental changes. For example, a single-issue campaign might broaden out to take on related issues.

Conscious

It is common to find that a group is not particularly conscious of the "decisions" it makes when it is first starting out. For example, the group might form with a "feeling" of affinity and shared purpose and never discuss things like its aims, purpose and values. A feeling of shared purpose is a strong glue holding people together, but it has its weaknesses. Conscious conversations usually end up with a clearer shared understanding, which can avoid the bad feeling and wasted time involved in disappointed expectations and misunderstandings.

The same is true for more practical decisions. Groups can slide into habits which shape how the group works without consciously making agreements. For example, if the same person sends out emails and manages social media for a group over a period of time, they may in effect become the "communications officer" without the group deciding they want one person in this role. Having a conscious conversation about how to organise communications means it's possible to consider the implications of different options and choose the one that works best.

Conscious agreements are also easier to communicate to the rest of the world and to new members (see "Appendix One: Declarations"). This can help the stability of the group as well. In the case of the "communications officer" example, all the conversations about how the role works will be useful notes and guidance if someone else takes over the job.

Less conscious decision-making can tend to favour the people who are already most empowered in a group. For example, someone who has a lot of confidence is more likely to explain how they think the group works to new people. Even if other people have different ideas that person's explanations may start to define how, in fact, the group works.

However, conscious and explicit decision-making can *also* favour the people who are already most empowered (see "Appendix One: Decision-Making Procedures"). These people may be more likely to put forward their views, more likely to fight if their ideas are opposed, and more likely to assume that their suggestion was agreed to if no one spoke against it. When these suggestions are written down as policy, or passed on to new people when they join, they look like the group consensus, even if not everyone was happy with them.

Conscious conversations about policy or group aims require that extra care is taken to be accessible. More people are likely to respond to "Shall I check the group email account?" than "What guidelines do we need for the 'communications officer' role?" The second question is easier for people to provide input on if they already have a lot of experience in groups. Plus, this second question is more abstract, which works better for some people than others. Using concrete examples and every-day language can help a wider range of people participate. This in turn means the agreements are shaped by more members of the group, in a more genuinely consensual way.

Key Areas of Constitutionalising

Exactly what questions a group needs to work out will depend on its context. For example, in a workers' co-op that provides its members with a wage it will be important to work out how to reach decisions that everyone finds fair. In this scenario the decisions will have a fundamental impact on people's liveli-hoods. In a community bring-and-share meal there may be a lot less decision-making required, and the decisions them-selves will affect people a lot less. In this case, the group may never agree on a decision-making method and may simply have an informal chat at the end of the meal if an issue comes up, for example, when to have the next meal!

However, the five areas discussed below cover the bases for most groups.

What Is the Group?

Sample questions: What is the purpose and what are the aims of the group? What principles and values do we share? What do we need to do to achieve our aims? Who can join the group?

These questions are at the foundations of any group. However, it is very common for a new group to dive into "doing stuff" without taking time to think about these questions. For example, if neighbours get together to fight gentrification in their area, they might assume that the reasons were obvious. But they could get a much clearer picture of where everyone is at by asking questions with fairly concrete answers like: "What are examples of the things we want to stop?" "What impacts will these things have, and which ones are we worried about?" This conversation would give a much clearer picture of how much people had in common and could provide the basis for setting out the purpose and values of the group.

How Are Decisions Made?

Sample questions: How does the group make decisions (e.g., by consensus, by voting)? Who needs to be involved in what kind of decisions? What decisions need to be made at regular meetings and what can be decided outside of those meetings?

Decision-making is critical to how a group puts its values into practice. For example, a network that exists to support local groups affected by the same issues might have the empowerment of those local groups as one of its core aims. It would be contradictory to then have a top-down decision-making structure, where a central committee in the network tells the local groups what to do. Instead, important decisions in the network might be made by representatives or delegates of all the local groups coming together a few times a year. The network might also decide that each local group has complete autonomy to do what they want, provided that no one uses the network's name to do things that go against core shared policies.

How Do We Get Things Done?

Sample questions: How often do we meet? Are there regular social events? How do we communicate among ourselves outside of meetings? How do we communicate with those not part of the group? Are sub-groups or individuals responsible for certain tasks?

The practices (or institutions) a group sets up to get things done could range from a monthly meeting, through to having nominated signatories on the bank account, to holding a regular stall in town on Saturdays (see "Appendix One: Institutions"). It could also include how the group socialises—having a bring-and-share meal to start each meeting or going on trips to national gatherings of people interested in the same issues.

The answers to these questions have a big impact on the experience of being part of the group, and how effectively things get done. Talking about how to organise can help a group find systems that are appropriate for its purpose and for the people involved. For example, many groups default to deciding everything in whole group meetings and splitting up tasks in an *ad hoc* way because it seems more egalitarian, when a well-thought-through working-group system could in some ways be equally democratic and more efficient. Groups also often default into socialising in the pub after meetings, and members don't think about more inclusive ways of getting to know one another. Ideally, group practices should reflect the members' aims and principles. For example, if a co-op aims to promote cooperation, in line with core cooperative principles, it might join regional and national cooperative networks and work collectively to strengthen the whole movement (see "Part Two: How to Build Durable Coalitions").

What Policies Do We Need?

Sample questions: How will we respond if someone makes a complaint to the group? Can we introduce rules that make the group safer to be in, for example, a commitment to supporting anyone who feels harassed or bullied? Is there a system that would make it harder for someone to steal group funds?

A policy doesn't need to be a five-page document in carefully crafted legalese (see "Appendix One: Rules"). It could include unwritten rules like not letting dogs use the allotment as a toilet. In other situations, it is important to have written policies that are worded carefully and to make sure everyone knows about them. Big public events often require that everyone reads and agrees to the safer spaces policy before entering. Co-ops will often have a "complaints", or "disciplinary and grievance policy" that makes it clear what behaviours are totally unacceptable, and what processes should be in place before a member is asked to leave.

This area is particularly sensitive, because there is a high risk that people will experience these rules and policies as restrictive or even oppressive. It is also difficult to make a rule which fits all situations and recognises everyone's needs. It can help if people recognise that a policy isn't usually chosen because it is the only right way to do things, but because it is a way that everyone can agree on. For example, there are many systems for sharing the cleaning in a communal house, and many different ideas about what it means to be clean enough. Coming to basic agreements about the housework can ease a lot of tension, especially if the agreements are reviewed when new people join.

How Can We Make the Group Empowering?

Sample questions: Are there particular groups of people who are likely to be disproportionately empowered or disempowered in the group? Can we introduce "checks and balances" to make it more difficult for individuals or sub-groups to gain too much influence? What can we do to make it easier for people who are currently marginalised to take on roles and help shape the group?

We join groups to achieve, or resist, more than we could individually. To make empowerment a reality, it needs to inform all the other areas involved in "constitutionalising". Making decision-making as democratic as possible is an obvious example. Other examples include creating systems to reduce the barriers to people getting involved, like paying baby-sitters so single parents can attend more easily, or choosing a venue that is as widely accessible as possible. Similarly, maximising empowerment can shape the aims of the group. For example, a trade union could prioritise issues affecting the lowest paid and most precarious workers. Linking up with like-minded groups can also help.

The priorities of each group will depend on its situation and members, so it is useful to start by thinking through any dynamics that are specific to your context. If a homeless action group includes "allies" who are securely housed there will need to be careful thought about potential power dynamics between them and the homeless people in the group. For example, you will need to think carefully about who speaks for the group in public, who has access to group resources, and whose views shape decision-making most. Similarly, in a project with a big budget, the finance team could easily end up with more than their fair share of influence over decision-making. Steps to ensure that everyone has a basic understanding of the financial situation could help balance that power (and help the whole group make better decisions overall).

There are practical tips on maximising empowerment in the section "Building an Empowering Culture" below.

The Importance of Group Culture

The success of all agreements depends as much on group culture as on what the agreements actually are. The culture is the moral norms, habits, attitudes and behaviours of the group. It is partly shaped by the rules a group makes, but not exclusively. For example, a group might introduce a grievance and conflict policy to encourage group members to raise issues with the whole group, or with the people concerned, rather than complaining to their friends or simply leaving. This policy will only work if people are prepared to raise issues and if they receive a constructive response when they do. In other words, it will only work if the group culture supports the policy.

An individual cannot simply decide what culture the group should have, but it is not totally beyond our collective control. Individuals can help build a culture that is in line with the agreements they have made, but the outcome will be shared. In the case of the conflict policy, individuals could model the process with a minor issue, make an effort to ensure that all sides are supported when a conflict does come up and ask direct questions if someone seems unhappy. The group can choose practices which help build the culture they want. For example, including a "niggles and appreciations" session as a standard item in a meeting or regular debriefs about how it is to work together can help build a culture that is more open about and accepting of conflict.

Putting It into Practice

The process of creating and maintaining empowering agreements and rules comes with some challenges. All the above general tips on how to run effective and participatory meetings apply (see also worksheets in Appendix Two and "Further Reading": Seeds for Change, *A Consensus Handbook* and *Effective Groups*). Below, we've fleshed out some of the specific challenges of constitutionalising and included some suggestions for how to deal with them.

The Process of "Constitutionalising"

If rule-making is to be based on consent, the process of making and reviewing the rules and agreements needs to be genuinely participatory. This can be challenging in a number of ways: it takes time; sometimes talking a lot about *how* to do things is off-putting for task-focused people who want to get things done; abstract conversations can be alienating.

Here are some concrete ideas for making the process of forming a group as genuinely inclusive as possible, bearing in mind these challenges:

- Take it one step at a time. Hold meetings which combine a couple of practical agenda items with one or two questions about how you want the group to work. This will help task-focused people stay engaged in the group.
- Make the discussions as context-based as possible so that there are more people who engage with the need to discuss the questions. For example, "Let's have a social media presence" could be combined with "What shall we put in the 'about us' section?" (What is the group? What are our principles?)
- Use concrete details (a) to make the discussion more accessible and (b) to check you aren't talking at cross-purposes. For example, when you say the community shop will promote "local" food do you mean food from a ten-mile radius or a hundred-mile radius?
- If the group doesn't address every question at the very beginning, look for opportunities later. More people are likely to engage in reviewing how things work once something has gone wrong. Alternatively, signal that you want to prioritise big discussions at the beginning of meetings.
- Split-up tasks. It may be that there are some things people can consent to, even if they weren't involved in drawing them up. For example, small groups could take on the task of writing one policy each, and then the whole group could suggest fundamental changes. By contrast, everyone might want to be involved together in deciding on a question like "What's the purpose of the group?"

New Members Joining

If new people join after all the agreements about the group have already been made, there is usually much less scope for them to have input into what those decisions should be. This poses some risks. The new people may experience those agreements as rules imposed from the outside and either feel resentful or simply ignore them because they never got a chance to shape them. Sometimes new members never find out about previous agreements or the reasons for them which can lead to carefully thought-out systems sliding into disuse, or the new person is only told when they've done something wrong, which is disempowering.

Bearing these challenges in mind here are a few techniques groups can use to integrate new members:

- When new people join, key points can be explained at the first meeting they attend. Whenever possible this can include an explanation of why the group arrived at the agreement in the first place. For example: "We use consensus decision-making, which means we discuss each item until we arrive at a way forward that everyone can accept. We believe that this shows the most respect for each person involved and encourages us all to participate in a cooperative mindset". Giving reasons can help new people understand and respect the group's agreements. New people can also be invited to give feedback on how the agreements work for them and be told if there is any possibility of changing them.
- More formal groups such as workers or housing co-ops often have an induction process and probation period to determine whether or not the new person and the co-op are right for each other. Of course, in this situation, there is a massive power imbalance between the established members (who already have a secure job/home) and the new members who are dependent on the others deciding

whether they are in or out. The relationship will be a little more balanced if new members understand the criteria they are being judged by, how the decisions will be made, and where they can go for support.

- In all groups, it is good to make sure that new members know how they can suggest changes to the ways the group operates. As well as simply explaining the processes ("This is how to put something on the agenda"), try inviting feedback. For example: "Here are all the things we do to try to make our events accessible, do you have any tips to improve it?"; or "Let's take ten minutes at the end of the meeting to hear how it worked for everyone. It'd be especially good to hear from people who've joined more recently because you'll be able to see everything with fresh eyes".

Regular Review of the Agreements

Agreements a group arrives at in the first few weeks of getting together might become less appropriate as the circumstances change and new members join. Therefore, for practical reasons as well as democratic ones, everything about a group needs to be open to review. At the same time, there are benefits to stability and groups protecting the core of what they are about.

Change is a common area of conflict in groups, because the process can be draining and/or because established members are resistant.

- Respect that people sometimes have strong feelings about change on all sides. Take time to understand the reasons why a policy was originally established, as well as why people want to change it.
- Instead of assuming that the existing agreement stays until everyone is ready to change it, try looking for new solutions which work for everyone. This might be not be

the suggested change or the old system, but something else entirely.

- Some people will find it easier to review agreements in answer to a broad question like: "How well is this group working for you". This will allow them to discuss the aspects that are most relevant to them.
- Alternatively, try having a rotation of areas to review as a regular part of group meetings. This could mean that different topics are covered more systematically, leading to better attendance than a "let's review our policies" meeting.

Building an Empowering Culture

Groups usually need to work on building a culture that puts their values into practice. We live in a society where power is very unevenly distributed, and power imbalances in our groups can be deeply entrenched. Prioritising empowerment in the constitutionalising process is a good start. Here are a few ideas groups have tried to build a more empowering culture:

- Sometimes unhealthy power dynamics can shift simply by varying the contexts in which group members interact. Not everyone thrives in meetings. Seeing other sides of each other can build more rounded relationships which make the meetings healthier. Try getting together to do the chores, paint a banner, construct an access ramp for the office, or attend a self-defence class. Or do things just for the sake of socialising. As with many things, variety is key, because we all have very different comfort zones.
- Changes in the distribution of the workload in the group may help more people feel actively involved and able to shape the group. Try regular skill-shares and buddying to make it easier for people to take on new roles. Have several people involved in every influential role so no one

person takes over or becomes indispensable. Devise rotas and jobs lists to rotate unpopular tasks.

- Talking about power directly can help to identify issues, to build understanding and to explore new ways of working. These conversations can be uncomfortable for everyone, but there is a risk of the biggest emotional burden falling on the people who are already marginalised. People who are affected by similar issues can get together to share perspectives on how the group affects them and to support each other through the process of raising issues. People who are more empowered can also work to build relationships with those who are not but who are supportive of them. The aim is to help everyone understand and to recognise the issues that are being raised, so as not to increase defensiveness.

- Tools that groups use to shift power dynamics include the practice of "calling out" which involves challenging oppressive behaviour. "Calling in" delivers this same challenge in a supportive way. "Calling in" has the benefit that the person being challenged may find it easier to hear and change their behaviour. Be aware though that requiring each other to use this approach gives the message that it is only okay to raise issues that affect you if you can be polite about it. Another tool is "step up, step back", which encourages people to reflect on the space they are taking up in the group and either put themselves forward more or take a step back as the case may be. This could also involve encouraging other people to take a step back if self-reflection isn't working.

In conclusion, setting up and maintaining a group will always be an experiment, and one that constantly changes as people join and leave and the external circumstances in which the group operates shift. One of the best tools a group has is the willingness to reflect on how things are going and to try out new ideas to address issues. This first part of the book is not a one stop shop. Constitutionalising is a process that continues for as long as the group does.

PART TWO

How to Build Durable Coalitions

How can we build and maintain popular, egalitarian movements capable of bringing about positive change? All too often, movements enjoy a brief explosion of activity and then fizzle out due to burn-out, conflict or because they just don't have enough people to keep up the work in the long term.

Effective coalitions, networks and alliances of groups can be an important ingredient in creating movements that are more effective, as well as supporting their member groups. Networks have the potential to enable:

- **Collective power:** Groups can usually achieve more in combination than in isolation. For example, the UK anti-fracking campaign would be a lot less effective if each community simply fought in its own corner. By supporting each other and co-ordinating the campaign, they have a chance of beating back the industry.
- **Solidarity:** Coalitions create a setting where groups working on different issues can reinforce each other, share resources and build trust among people affected by different issues. For example, groups in the same town working on issues like housing, migration, racial justice and feminism can network, and offer each other resources or practical help to boost each campaign.
- **Sustaining momentum:** Because coalitions involve more people than a single group, they have the potential to make both the network and the individual groups involved, more durable. All groups have peaks and

troughs of activity. When members' energy is sapped, some disband entirely. A healthy coalition should be able to keep going even if the member groups change.

- **Seeds of a new society:** Coming together in networks of groups is a practical way of experimenting with different ways of organising. Coalitions create spaces to practice cooperative, anti-hierarchical ways of working, just like separate groups do, but on a larger and more complex scale. They are a more effective and realistic model for building social alternatives and can be more durable.

This durability is not without problems, and networks often experience problems created by power imbalances and exclusions, just like smaller groups. This second part focuses on how networks and coalitions can put cooperative and anti-hierarchical principles into practice—building collective power while guarding against the tendency for an individual or sub-group to dominate the others. The aim is to create a strong network that both achieves its immediate goals, and acts as a potential model for a different way of organising society.

Assuming you've already got a group up and running, what follows will be of most interest to groups newly coming together to form a coalition or network. Existing coalitions could also use this part of the guide if they want to review how they are working together. It might also be relevant to a large group that is sub-divided into different teams—for example, a large housing cooperative with multiple households.

The sorts of questions we respond to here are: What is a coalition? What particular challenges do you face? How will you organise yourselves? How will you make decisions? How will you share information? What policies and rules do you need?

A core element of anarchic "constitutionalising" is balancing power between different players (individual or group) so that the group or coalition as a whole supports everyone's empowerment, and no one is able to dominate others because of the way the coalition is set up. Guarding against domination is a key concern of *anarchic agreements*, and this is as important in designing coalitions as is the case with groups. Having a shared agreement won't prevent the abuse of power. However, the process of creating agreements helps build trust and promote dialogue about how to curb abuses. Agreements and constitutions are tools to help create empowering collaborative cultures, but they are not substitutes for them.

Challenges for Coalitions

The process of coming together as a coalition has a lot in common with coming together as a group of individuals. However, coalitions are usually larger and more complex than groups, and as such the challenges involved can be amplified. The following three areas pose particular difficulties for coalitions that want to be empowering:

- building trust and relationships;
- navigating difference;
- accessibility.

Building Trust and Relationships

Compared to a group, coalitions usually involve a much smaller proportion of people forming direct personal relationships. It is likely that lots of the people involved will never meet. For example, most member groups will probably only send a few people to each coalition meeting. Even if everyone is there, meetings are likely to be larger with less scope for informal interactions, and decision-making is less likely to be directly democratic.

Without direct personal relationships, it is much harder to create a "feeling" of common purpose and to understand each other's priorities and differences. These things are all essential to building a cohesive group. More people are empowered to participate when they feel comfortable with the people involved. Trust also makes it easier to address power issues without creating conflicts—and it's easier to address any conflicts that do arise without them becoming "stuck" or toxic! Therefore, even if a coalition gives high priority to equality in their agreements, it may be harder to build trust in practice.

Navigating Difference

Groups that form a coalition often have less in common with each other than the individuals in the various groups. Members of groups are likely to have some close connections—for example, people may live or work together, or campaign on the same issue. Coalitions are often broader. A food bank, an allotment association, and a parents' campaign for better school dinners might all be tackling "food poverty", but they may not have much else in common!

Difference isn't (necessarily) the same as incompatibility! It can be a source of strength. The food bank, allotment association and school dinner campaign might all learn a lot from each other. However, sometimes differences *will* make things difficult, and it may be better to acknowledge this and keep the work separate, rather than waste energy papering over disagreements. Even if groups have enough in common to be able to work together, unacknowledged differences can lead to conflicts, or slow things down because communications get bogged down in misunderstandings.

Critically, differences like social class can also be a source of power imbalances, giving one sub-set of people an advantage over others. It's important to be open to the dynamics in your coalition, and to think creatively about how advantages and disadvantages can be addressed.

Because this is such a critical area, we have outlined some of the many types of difference a coalition may need to negotiate, and some of the impacts those differences can have.

- **Purpose and values:** A coalition that comes together for short-term, pragmatic reasons may be made up of member groups which have conflicting purposes and values. For example, anglers, kayakers, and environmentalists might all be opposed to a specific hydro-electric scheme—but still be opposed to a lot of what each other stand for! Even longer-term coalitions may be made up of groups with very different priorities. For example, numerous groups might be working together under a "social justice" banner in a given town, but uniting against something is not the same as reaching an agreement about possible solutions to the problem. If you are coming together for short-term pragmatic reasons, but have very different values, it is best to acknowledge this and take it into account in your agreements. Finding equitable balances of values, as well as of power, is part of the challenge of coalition building.
- **Group culture:** Groups in a coalition are likely to have different ways of making decisions, different norms around how they hold meetings, and different expectations about how groups are structured. This can lead to a lot of misunderstandings and frustration. It can also exacerbate power dynamics among sub-groups. For example, if one group imposes its norms on everyone else, it becomes more difficult for other people to join in meetings. "Imposing" in this context rarely involves consciously telling everyone else what to do! It may involve the opposite. If a group with a lot of informal power simply continues to do things in its habitual "way" without explaining what it's doing, the result can be a coalition culture that is alienating for many members.
- **Strategy and tactics:** Groups may enter into coalition with very different ideas about how to tackle their shared problem. For example, a campaigning coalition may involve groups with distinct focuses, ranging from lobbying through awareness raising to direct action. This can

be a sign that the groups in the coalition have different experiences, values, or long-term goals. These should be explored openly so that member groups can work in coalition without compromising each other's aims. Even if the groups have very similar values, they still need to work out how to combine different tactics into an effective strategy.

- **Resources:** It is particularly challenging to operate as empowered equals when some groups have access to a lot more resources than others. For example, this could be material resources. If a non-governmental organisation (NGO) enters into coalition with voluntary community groups, the NGO may be able to put their paid staff into roles like outreach and media and gain disproportionate influence over campaign messaging. Or the resources may be less tangible. For example, in a network of different geographically based communities, a group based in a neighbourhood full of retired middle-class people may have a lot of members with time and privilege enabling them to shape the direction and culture of the coalition.

Accessibility

A coalition may have more scope than a small group to pool resources to make their meetings more accessible, for example, paying a bit extra for a step-free venue, or having same-language sub-groups and interpreters in a multilingual setting. However, coalitions may generate more barriers simply because they are larger. This might not always be about things that completely exclude someone from attending or participating. There are also factors which increase the effort required to get involved or feel like you are being heard, which can mean that some people are effectively excluded.

Because coalitions are likely to involve more people—possibly also more people who don't know each other—some people are likely to find meetings intimidating and draining. If the coalition is operating over a large geographical area, attending face-to-face meetings involves time and travel, and can be difficult in terms of costs, physical and mental health, mobility issues, juggling other responsibilities, etc. This is also likely to mean longer meetings to make it worth the travel time, which also poses difficulties in terms of energy, overnight stays, childcare, and so on.

The complexity of coalitions poses challenges too. The amount of information that people have to get their heads around can be overwhelming. Large groups often involve intricate systems and policies, for sub-dividing tasks and administration, and so are more likely to have formal procedures that are unfamiliar or feel bureaucratic to newcomers.

Coalitions may be especially appealing to people who have a lot of ambition to make a big impact. In itself, this kind of ambition can result in positive change in the world. However, because of the way organisations are usually set up, there is a high potential for coalitions to generate a small extremely motivated elite who are difficult to get hold of. But no one has all the answers. Networks are only ever as strong as the sum of their parts (but sometimes they are stronger), so it is important to balance ambition with care and attention to the accessibility and internal democracy of the network, ensuring some people don't end up gaining power at the expense of others.

Constitutionalising: Key Questions

We have broken down the core areas that groups in a coalition need to address to work out how, and how much they will work together. The questions we have suggested could be used to structure your meetings. In practice, there is an overlap between the sections, and you may need to re-visit your first decisions as you go through the process. Each coalition should consider the specifics of its situation, to work out which system best suits its needs in terms of empowerment, sustainability, and effectiveness. As well as being a useful exercise in and of itself, the process of working through these questions will help to build trust and stronger relationships, as members get to know each other better.

To recap from part one, we suggest that the process of agreement should be based on a commitment to three key concepts:

1 **Conscious:** Explicitly discussing things and coming to conscious decisions about how to work together allows more space for everyone to contribute. By contrast, if you simply allow group practices to "evolve" this can easily lead to informal hierarchies that are hard to challenge.

2 **Consensual:** Any rules or ways of working are collectively agreed upon and not imposed on anyone against their will. When new groups join, any existing agreements are clearly explained, verbally or in writing, so that their members understand the coalition's core values.

3 **Changeable:** Agreements can change over time as circumstances or group membership changes. In this way, any agreements continue to have everyone's conscious consent, and are not dictated by founding members.

What Is the Coalition?

This is the core question which will shape everything else. It is worth spending time exploring this question. If you come up with an answer that really works, then your collaborations are much more likely to be empowering and sustainable.

This sequence of questions should help you through the process.

What Do You Have in Common?

It can help to start by looking at all the groups and working out what things you have in common—finding the overlap between your different campaigns and projects will help you see how you can strengthen and support each other.

It is also important to recognise your differences.

Respectfully acknowledging and exploring differences can make them less divisive, rather than more. It gives you the information you need to create agreements about how to work together that make sense. Open dialogue about your disagreements, fears, or concerns also makes it harder for opponents to exploit them to undermine you.

- **Goals:** Consider the long- and short-term aims of different groups. For example, a short-term aim that environmental groups could share might be eliminating plastic. Longer term, some of those groups may be working towards a total restructuring of social and economic practices, while others might simply want some reforms within the current system. Think through what impact these differences might have on working together, how wide they are and how you can make collaboration work for everyone.
- **Values:** What principles do you all hold? Are there some values that are central to some groups and acceptable to others? For example, a coalition that included some animal rights groups could incorporate veganism into the things they did together, even if it isn't a priority for all of the groups. Do you have any clashes in values? If you use the same words to describe your values, say a commitment to equality, do you mean the same thing by this?
- **Experiences:** Sometimes a coalition will be specifically for groups of people who share particular experiences. For example, users of national health mental health services might have mutual aid groups for people with particular diagnoses and come together in a coalition to campaign for better provision. Also think about how your experiences can be transformed into tools to support others.

What Do You Want to Achieve by Working Together?
It's useful to be clear about what your purpose is in coming together as a coalition. Different coalitions will have different

levels of priority on goals, values and shared experiences. Therefore, you could end up with a pragmatic alliance based on a very specific goal, such as challenging a particularly repressive police behaviour that affects all your campaigns. At the other end of the spectrum, a coalition could be built around shared values of collaboration and mutual aid and a desire to put them into practice for their own sake. Or your purpose might be the empowerment of people who share a particular experience, regardless of whether you hold the same views or want to do the same things.

Being clear about why you are working together will help determine what form your network should take, how closely you should collaborate, and how much care you need to take to make sure member groups keep their autonomy.

What Capacity Do You Have for Working Together?
The reality is that working in a coalition takes time and energy. Even if it is more efficient in the long run to share resources and tasks among different groups, the process of setting up the coalition will require a lot of commitment in the short term. You will need time to arrive at agreements and set up systems—and to learn how to communicate and work together. Is it realistic to do that immediately? Generally, the more closely you plan to work together, the more time you need to get to know each other and to work out how you will work together.

How Closely Do You Want to Work Together?
This question is best addressed once you've thought about all questions above. The coalition is likely to be more sustainable and powerful if you collaborate in ways that make sense for your situation. Ideally, that means it needs to work for everyone, and not just be driven by a few keen individuals.

Remember that the answer can change over time. Perhaps initially you just want to organise occasional skill-shares for members of the different groups, while remaining open to collaborating more closely as you get to know each other better. If the main barrier is a lack of capacity, could groups which have more time to shoulder the burden of any background administrative work offer to organise meetings or manage a website?

What Particular Challenges Do You Face?

As well as focusing on what you want to achieve, it is worth working out if there are particular factors which will make it harder for you to sustainably work together as empowered equals and to offer each other practical solidarity and mutual aid. The list below of common challenges for coalitions provides a useful reference point: Are there any of these which are particularly significant for you to address? Getting clear about the most significant challenges from the outset will help you come up with agreements which address them.

- **Building trust and relationships:** Are there any particular reasons why trust-building might be challenging for your coalition? Are you geographically very spaced out, and lacking resources for face-to-face meetings? Do some member groups support causes that other member groups are wary of? How do you represent the voices of those who cannot be present? Are you operating in multiple languages, preventing lots of people in the network from speaking to each other without translation? Will the individuals who are part of member groups change frequently, meaning you need to build in ongoing opportunities for people to get to know each other? These kinds of trust barriers can be addressed in your agreements by committing to practical methods, for example, deciding who can speak for the group and how, how to manage the autonomy of member-groups, or creating same-language sub-groups, and investing in interpreters. Be prepared to devote time to getting to know each other and building relationships *before* coming to any decisions about how (and how much) you want to collaborate.

- **Navigating difference:** Consider the differences between and within the groups in your coalition. In what ways are they likely to give advantage to some people over others? For example, consider a migration-focused network, consisting of mutual aid groups for people seeking asylum, grant-funded campaigning NGOs and "activist" groups consisting of non-migrants wanting to offer solidarity. On the democratic principle of decisions being made by the people most affected by them (also known as *subsidiarity*), people with experience of seeking asylum might want to direct any campaigning on the issue. How can you make sure that your agreements about process and decision-making enable this?

- **Resources:** Resource differences are another problem. Coalitions can take a substantial step towards balancing power between member groups by redistributing resources internally. For example, what could be achieved by better resourced groups lending out equipment, offering free venues or sharing their media contacts? Be clear about the terms of this aid to avoid anyone in those groups calling in unanticipated "favours" later on down the line. Think how the arrangements can be managed fairly and in the spirit of equality. For example, if an NGO is offering a paid member of staff to support the coalition, the coalition as a whole could be responsible for deciding what that person's priorities should be. Otherwise there is a risk of *increasing* inequalities within the network rather than re-balancing them.

- **Accessibility**: Are there access barriers to getting involved that are specific to your coalition? This could be barriers that all or most of you share, and that everyone probably knows you need to find solutions to. For example, a single parents' network will definitely need to think about child-care for meetings; a coalition of people claiming benefits will need to find a way to cover costs that doesn't involve people dipping into their own pockets. If you are running a national campaign that involves urgent decisions between face-to-face meetings, you will need to address any access barriers to online organising. Alternatively, the majority culture or practices of your coalition may be fine for most people who are currently involved, but not for others. For example, a network that formed through "protest camps" may run on the assumption that everyone owns camping equipment and is physically able to sleep in a tent and move around on rough ground. It is less straightforward to work out what are the most significant barriers for people who aren't involved in your coalition. By definition, the people at your meeting have not faced insurmountable barriers! Make space for people to talk about anything that discourages them from coming and take what they say seriously. Ask member groups to survey members who don't engage in the coalition to see what their reasons are.

How Will You Organise Yourselves?

This will depend very much on your purpose, and may change over time. Depending on how varied your purposes and groups are, and how closely you are working together, your work may be easier or harder to define. For example, if your only purpose is to provide a platform for member groups to help each other out when they need it, then the "work" may just be to maintain an online space or email list where people can communicate. If you are running a major project together then the actual tasks are likely to evolve as the project progresses, and may include collectively organising finances, publicity, social media accounts, meetings, and so on. This may involve building more sub-groups or committees, and finding ways of linking them into the coalitions (see "How Do You Organise Whole Group Decisions?" below).

How Will You Divide Work and Responsibilities?

You might try:

- **Specialised roles**: Individuals can be assigned to particular tasks like drawing up the annual accounts, compiling the monthly newsletter, etc. While the experience people develop through specialisation is invaluable for the durability of organisations, it can also quickly lead to new cliques. Thinking about how these roles can be filled is very important. Are they best filed by volunteers, should they be elected roles, appointed by committee, and/or rotated, with roles always filled by a different member group?
- **Sub-groups**: Working groups can take on particular areas of responsibility, for example, finances, publicity, etc. These working groups can be made open to anyone who wants to take part or organise a selection process, so as to consciously mix together people up from different member groups.
- **Rotation**: Some tasks can be regularly reassigned to individuals or member groups. For example, each group can take a turn to organise the coalition meeting. The best method will depend a lot on your situation. If you are low on capacity, then efficiency might be your biggest priority, and you might only have one individual in any specialised role. However, giving areas of responsibility to sub-groups could be better for the long-term sustainability of the coalition, because information and skills won't simply be lost if one person decides to leave. This would be especially important if you have a high turnover of members, or if it is necessary to ensure that different member groups are represented within each

area of responsibility. No arrangement is perfect so weigh up the pros and cons and make sure any working group structure is clearly explained to anyone new. It should be made easy for new people to join a group if they want to be involved, but how easy?

How Will You Make Decisions?

How much shared decision-making you do will also depend on your purposes and how closely you are working together. Most groups need to balance a need to get everyone's consent on important decisions with a need for efficiency and minimising time spent in meetings. Working out which decisions really need everyone's input, which can be delegated or represented, and who is entitled to decide (groups or individuals?) is critical to an effective coalition. "Everyone deciding everything" may sound democratic, but in reality it may be a recipe for very long and boring meetings that no one comes to! In practice, it may be better to apply a principle of decisions being made by people who are fundamentally affected by them (*subsidiarity* again). In this way, coalition-wide decision-making can be reserved for questions with a far-reaching impact like strategy or the annual budget, while day-to-day decision-making happens in working groups.

Consensus, Voting or Something in Between?

What decision-making method is right for your situation? This is likely to depend on the culture and values of member groups and how much member groups want to protect their autonomy. If empowerment of your members is a top priority, then you might want to go for the highest level of consensus possible. If your capacity is limited or you need to make a decision quickly in an urgent situation, then you might prioritise efficiency and simple majorities. It will depend on whether you think some activities should be subject to higher standards of consent than others. For example, members may make it hard for anyone to change the coalition's name or operate its social media or bank accounts but relatively easy to alter rules on conduct at meetings. Remember: decision-making procedures can have unintended consequences, constraining and enabling in unanticipated ways. These are some standard methods:

- **Consensus decision-making:** Issues are discussed until a way forward is found that everyone affected can consent to. Ideally, the group finds win-win solutions that everyone actively supports, although in practice some people will likely have reservations that they are prepared to set aside. Consensus allows for just one individual to block a decision from going ahead (one member, one veto). The yardstick for a block (or veto) is high—it needs to be a deep and fundamental objection, often described as "I would have to leave the group if this went ahead". Consensus allows for extensive discussion and the highest level of democratic control for everyone involved, but it also requires time for people to explore issues and think creatively about different solutions. This makes it essential that only the most important decisions go to the whole group. Difficulties in reaching consensus can create a bias towards the status quo—if you can't agree on how to change things, the default may be things staying as they are.

- **Simple majority vote:** Any proposal goes ahead if a majority of the people affected consent to it. This can have the benefit of speed and efficiency. It can also provide a way forward in a situation where it is important to do something, but you can't reach agreement on what! However, if proposals go ahead despite fundamental objections this can be damaging in the long run, creating large, disaffected minorities, so think carefully about the impacts of this option.

- **Super majority vote:** In this method decisions will go ahead if they are backed by a high majority—how high will depend on how important the decision is, or on its strategic purpose. For some decisions this could be as low as 60 percent. Others only allow for one block to be disregarded (consensus-minus-one). Radical Routes (see "Appendix One: Decision-Making Procedures") has a rule where one block for every twelve member groups can be over-turned (effectively a 90 percent supermajority, but of co-ops, not individuals). Some groups use a super majority vote of all members as a back-up, for example, if three successive meetings have failed to reach consensus on a proposal.

How Do You Organise Whole Group Decisions?

If you want your coalition to work with the consent of all its members, then you need to be able to get everyone's involvement in major decisions—at least all those who want to be involved. This isn't straightforward, but large groups of all kinds have developed a variety of methods to make it possible.

- **Spokescouncils:** Issues are discussed in member groups, which then each appoint a delegate. These delegates (or spokespeople) come together to report back to the "hub" on what the different member groups have said and to start exploring options they think might be acceptable to all groups. Once they have a good option (or a range of options), they take it back to the member groups. At this stage, member groups can either agree to the option, suggest amendments or ask for additional changes. The delegates/spokespeople then meet a second time to report on what has come from their groups and look for amendments or new proposals that will make the decision acceptable to everyone. This back and forth process continues until a decision is reached. This process can be time-consuming and requires a high level of skill and self-awareness from spokespeople, to ensure they are genuinely representing their group and not just themselves in the spokespeople meetings. It also gives the highest possible degree of power to member groups.

- **General meetings:** This is a meeting which anyone within the coalition can attend as an individual. It might split into small groups for discussion, but actual decision-making is done with everyone present. This cuts out the back and forth and reporting of others' views involved in spokescouncil meetings. However, there are often a smaller proportion of people who feel empowered to contribute to large group discussions. Also, once a meeting gets past a certain size, it can be hard to hear each other, even with microphones.

- **Remote organising:** Up to a point, people can contribute to decision-making online. For example, a sub-group could draw up a survey to sound out large numbers of people on an issue before creating a proposed way forward. There are online platforms, like *Loomio*, that are specially designed for anti-hierarchical groups to explore issues and come to decisions (see www.loomio.org). Theoretically, online communications should be more accessible than travelling to meet in person. However, pay attention to what proportion of your group actually participates in whatever method you use, and if it is always the same people. In practice, you may find that more people attend and contribute at face-to-face meetings. For many groups, remote organising works well for straightforward decisions, but face-to-face meetings are still needed for anything contentious or complex.

Who Are the Decision-Making Members?

As a coalition of groups, you need to decide whether people participate in decision-making as individuals, or as part of a block with the rest of their member group. This decision is more significant if you are using some kind of voting system—for example, do you need 90 percent of individuals to agree or 90 percent of member groups?

Having each member group operating as a voting "block" may be simplest structurally, but in practice it may be complicated. For example, what if individuals have divided loyalties, between the coalition and their own groups (or groups, if they are part of more than one)? This question gets more complicated still if the network is made up of a mix of groups and individuals. For example, if several communities opposing open cast coal mining come together, they may be joined by people who want to fight against coal mining, but don't have a potential mine or local group in their area.

Another factor is whether the member groups are a similar size, or have similar stake, in the decision being made. In a network of housing co-ops, should a large cooperative co-housing project with one hundred members have the same weight as a household of three people? Do you need to weight votes in some way?

How Will You Share Information?

First things, first: What information do you need to share? As a general principle, everyone should have access to information that enables them to participate as empowered members of the network—for example, information about finances, policies and how to contribute to setting an agenda and decision-making. There are practical things, too, like how to get hold of shared resources, how to access social media accounts or how to find out about public statements made in the coalition's name. This doesn't mean bombarding everyone with blow-by-blow accounts of everything that's going on; it means well-organised information that people can find when they need it.

This needs to be balanced with an awareness of data protection, whether for individual privacy (see: www.eugdpr. org), or because your group is likely to be under surveillance by the state or corporations. For example, if you publish meeting minutes online, how will you protect individuals from being identified?

What Communication Methods Can You Use?

Based on the principles above, think about what information should be sent to people (by email or social media) and what information should simply be there for people to access (in a shared online space, or an open access office). Make sure it is made as easy as possible for people to get information about how to participate in the coalition—how to put items on meeting agendas, get involved in working groups, etc. For example, create a new member induction pack and start each meeting with a quick run-down of what decision-making methods you use and how they work. Also consider what information needs to be circulated on a need-to-know basis—for example, member contacts should be held in a secure database that can only be accessed by the membership team.

What Policies and "Rules" Do You Need?

Many people are resistant to policies and "rules" in anti-hierarchical groups. However, all groups have rules. They might not be written down and can take the form of habits or inherited conventions. There are good reasons to make rules explicit, even if they remain informal. Policies and rules provide a way to consciously address issues like power and accessibility, which can often be invisible to people who don't experience marginalisation and exclusion. Having rules can also help arriving at agreements about what to do when things go wrong *before* a crisis hits. Another benefit of creating rules or policies is that you can create general responses to common problems, which means that you don't need to take every single question to a meeting. For example, if you have a food policy, then the kitchen team doesn't need to check the menu at every general meeting!

Exactly what policies you need will depend on your group situation, but what follows is a list of areas that are common to most groups.

Joining and Leaving

As a baseline, groups need to be free to leave the coalition if it no longer meets their needs. It is worth planning around this possibility from the start, for example, by making sure that the coalition isn't too dependent on any one sub-group or individual.

Not all coalitions are open to new members. If yours is, it is worth thinking through and being clear about your membership criteria before a new person or group asks to join. Make sure that any requirements for new members also apply to the established membership!!

There may also be situations where a coalition would want to ask a group to leave, for example, if they went against agreed core policies, or a group might want to leave or might have become inactive or defunct. Specifying in advance what the key rules are and the process followed when a group leaves will make it easier to address any issues that arise.

Conflict and Accountability Processes

Conflict can generate a lot of fear, and people are often reluctant to address it, but groups can fall apart if conflict is left unaddressed. Having a process in place can help people through; you may even require that people engage with that process as a condition of membership. This protects the coalition from situations where people are refusing to engage in conflict resolution (or nominally agreeing, but dragging their heels on practicalities like setting a date, with the impact being that the conflict isn't resolved!).

You may need different processes depending on the situation. Conflicts are not always straightforward disagreements or personality clashes between two "equal" sides. If someone has been assaulted, they are unlikely to want a "mediation" with the person who attacked them! Rather than a single conflict process, you may need a range of options depending on the dynamics of the situation, and whether the priority is to re-build relationships so people can go on working together, or to create more safety for someone who has been harmed.

What Do You Want to Support?

Creating coalition policies is an opportunity to learn new ways of operating, and to consciously create a different culture. You can deliberately adopt new practices that communicate your values to the world, often in a more powerful way than simply writing your mission statement on a website. Examples could include using open source software; using a Creative Commons or anti-copyright license for your resources; providing fair trade, sustainably sourced, vegan food for your events; buying from cooperatives wherever possible.

In sum, anti-oppression is a vital area for creating positive new practices in order to build a different culture. Social structures of oppression are deeply embedded in mainstream culture, and people inevitably carry them into the groups they join. Turning these patterns around takes a lot more than simply declaring yourselves opposed to discrimination and hierarchy. Policies are tools for change, both symbolic markers of commitment and benchmarks for improved practice. They should help you enact your principles and demonstrate that it is possible to put them into practice.

Building Your Coalition Culture

The agreements you make are only one element of building a coalition that is empowering and sustainable, especially if you are hoping to work in alternative ways, based on solidarity, mutual aid and liberation. The culture you create together is another vital ingredient. Culture is harder to pin down than a set of rules and agreements, but it can be just as empowering or disempowering. We focus here on some of the concrete and practical things you can do to create and maintain a healthy coalition culture. Some of these things could be considered when making agreements and policies, but we have given them their own section because it is so vital to put them into practice consistently, and not just to agree to them once and then forget about them!

- **Effective facilitation:** If people have a positive experience of participating in large meetings, they are more likely to stay actively involved in shaping the coalition. Good facilitation is about more than enabling focused, efficient decision-making. It creates space for different perspectives, different needs and access requirements, and different ways of thinking and contributing. Facilitation also plays a role in making sure people are welcomed to the space, and that everyone has the information they need in order to participate.
- **Space for reflection and feedback:** There is no one-size-fits-all set of rules for how to create an empowering space. However, creating space for people to reflect on and share their experiences of being part of the coalition will give you a wealth of information about how to change things, so that they work better for more people. Create a range of different formats for people to contribute, for example: training sessions, online discussion spaces, review meetings, even feedback forms. It is also easier to maintain a culture of accountability in the group when it is easy for individuals to give feedback. As such, working group meetings could also include a chance for people to review their experience of working together.
- **Social time:** For many people, this is an essential ingredient in building trusting relationships, and feeling able to participate. Longer or residential meetings (e.g.,

conferences) allow for people to spend informal time together, rather than just talking about what's on the agenda. Consider games, music or opportunities to do practical work together for people who find more structured social time easier than chatting. Be aware that longer or residential meetings won't be accessible to everyone, even if you provide childcare and travel bursaries. Can you also have regional get-togethers, working group meet-ups or even space for informal chat online to increase the range of people who feel connected?

- **Accessibility:** Accessibility needs to be an ongoing conversation, not something you tick off at the beginning of forming a coalition. Keep asking people about their access requirements when organising events. Existing members may have had a change of circumstance, and more people may have joined. As well as physical requirements like ramps and hearing aid induction loops, encourage people to share any requirements related to mental health, language barriers, neuro-divergence, childcare responsibilities, finances, etc. If you really want your meetings to be accessible, be prepared to give it a high priority in your budget and planning time, and think creatively about solutions.

- **Mutual support:** Thriving coalitions are often maintained by personal relationships in which people offer practical and emotional support. When these relationships are purely informal, they are often unfairly distributed. People with the skills to ask for what they need inevitably receive a lot more care, and people with the skills and willingness to offer end up shouldering an unfair burden of the emotional labour. Try experimenting with more structured ways of creating supportive relationships, for example, a mediation and listening team, a buddy system, peer support groups, or action learning sets.

Conclusion: Connections within a Wider Movement

Effective coalitions are important building blocks for social change. Connecting with other groups and networks opens avenues for practical solidarity and for forging strong, plural movements. It's easy to find examples of mutual aid in times of crisis: people habitually build coalitions to help each other out during floods or pandemics. What happens to these networks in the long term? The old authorities eventually step in, take over, initiate inquiries, write reports and do little. Building alternatives means learning to sustain and extend these experiments.

Building coalitions of groups provides an opportunity to learn about constitutionalising by doing it, by picking up new ideas and ways of looking at things from other perspectives and networks. We think of anarchic group- and coalition-building as an ongoing experiment which offers new ways of organising and of establishing enduring alternatives to top-down systems. It will have far greater reach if we share stories about what worked and what didn't with others and use those stories to inform future organising.

Sample Constitutions

In what follows we present sample constitutional texts taken from a range of anarchist and anarchistic groups. The choice of texts, and how we have edited them, seeks to reflect our claim that constitutions are designed to challenge global structures of power like capitalism, patriarchy and class through localised actions in local contexts. They do so by declaring that the group is against some perceived injustice or oppression and establishing rules, institutions and decision-making procedures that ensure those groups do not replicate the external power imbalances internally. The general principles are uniformly anti-oppression, anti-statist, anti-capitalist, and non-hierarchical. In other words, anarchy structures these groups. Anarchy is a constitutional norm or principle. These examples are not exhaustive, nor will they necessarily be appropriate to all groups, but they indicate possibilities, and we hope they will inspire you to experiment.

The collection is reprinted with the permission of each of the groups (where permission could be granted). For more examples of anarchist and anarchistic constitutions, and live weblinks to the cited documents, visit www.anarchyrules.info.

1. Declarations

Declarations are statements that bring the group into being by setting out who they are and what they're for.

a. The Preamble to the Constitution of the Industrial Workers of the World (1905)

The IWW is a revolutionary syndicalist union, with strong affiliations to the anarchist movement. It counted Lucy Parsons among its founding members. This preamble has been amended only once since it was first ratified in 1905—to add the line "and live in harmony with the Earth".

The working class and the employing class have nothing in common. There can be no peace so long as hunger and want are found among millions of the working people and the few, who make up the employing class, have all the good things of life.

Between these two classes a struggle must go on until the workers of the world organise as a class, take possession of the means of production, abolish the wage system, and live in harmony with the Earth.

We find that the centering of the management of industries into fewer and fewer hands makes the trade unions unable to cope with the ever growing power of the employing class. The trade unions foster a state of affairs which allows one set of workers to be pitted against another set of workers in the same industry, thereby helping defeat one another in wage wars. Moreover, the trade unions aid the employing class to mislead the workers into the belief that the working class have interests in common with their employers.

These conditions can be changed and the interest of the working class upheld only by an organisation formed in such a way that all its members in any one industry, or in all industries if necessary, cease work whenever a strike or lockout is on in any department thereof, thus making an injury to one an injury to all.

Instead of the conservative motto, "A fair day's wage for a fair day's work", we must inscribe on our banner the revolutionary watchword, "Abolition of the wage system".

It is the historic mission of the working class to do away with capitalism. The army of production must be organised, not only for everyday struggle with capitalists, but also to carry on production when capitalism shall have been overthrown. By organising industrially we are forming the structure of the new society within the shell of the old.

b. Emma Goldman, "A New Declaration of Independence", Published in *Mother Earth* 4 no. 4, (July 1909)

Goldman discusses how she came to write this alternative declaration in her autobiography, Living My Life *(New York: Dover Publications 1970 [1931]), 455. It is available online at the Emma Goldman Papers, https://www.lib.berkeley.edu/goldman/.*

When, in the course of human development, existing institutions prove inadequate to the needs of man, when they serve merely to enslave, rob, and oppress mankind, the people have the eternal right to rebel against, and overthrow, these institutions.

The mere fact that these forces—inimical to life, liberty, and the pursuit of happiness—are legalized by statute laws, sanctified by divine rights, and enforced by political power, in no way justifies their continued existence.

We hold these truths to be self-evident: that all human beings, irrespective of race, color, or sex, are born with the equal right to share at the table of life; that to secure this right, there must be established among men economic, social, and political freedom; we hold further that government exists but to maintain special privilege and property rights; that it coerces man into submission and therefore robs him of dignity, self-respect, and life.

The history of the American kings of capital and authority is the history of repeated crimes, injustice, oppression, outrage, and abuse, all aiming at the suppression of individual liberties and the exploitation of the people. A vast country, rich enough to supply all her children with all possible comforts, and ensure well-being to all, is in the hands of a few, while the nameless millions are at the mercy of ruthless wealth gatherers, unscrupulous lawmakers, and corrupt politicians. Sturdy sons of America are forced to tramp the country in a fruitless search for bread, and many of her daughters are driven into the street, while thousands of tender children are daily sacrificed on the altar of Mammon. The reign of these kings is holding mankind in slavery, perpetuating poverty and disease, maintaining crime and corruption; it is fettering the spirit of liberty, throttling the voice of justice, and degrading and oppressing humanity. It is engaged in continual war and slaughter, devastating the country and destroying the best and finest qualities of man; it nurtures superstition and ignorance, sows prejudice and strife, and turns the human family into a camp of Ishmaelites.

We, therefore, the liberty-loving men and women, realizing the great injustice and brutality of this state of affairs, earnestly and boldly do hereby declare, That each and every individual is and ought to be free to own himself and to enjoy the full fruit of his labor; that man is absolved from all allegiance to the kings of authority and capital; that he has, by the very fact of his being, free access to the land and all means of production, and entire liberty of disposing of the fruits of his efforts; that each and every individual has the unquestionable and unabridgeable right of free and voluntary association with other equally sovereign individuals for economic, political, social, and all other purposes, and that to achieve this end man must emancipate himself from the sacredness of property, the respect for man-made law, the fear of the Church, the cowardice of public opinion, the stupid arrogance of national, racial, religious, and sex superiority, and from the narrow puritanical conception of human life. And for the support of this Declaration, and with a firm reliance on the harmonious blending of man's social and individual tendencies, the lovers of liberty joyfully consecrate their uncompromising devotion, their energy and intelligence, their solidarity and their lives.

This "Declaration" was written at the request of a certain newspaper, which subsequently refused to publish it, though the article was already in composition.

c. The Principles of Solidarity and the Declaration of the Occupation of New York City

Occupy Wall Street was not an explicitly anarchist movement but Mark Bray reports that almost 40 percent of the original organisers identified as anarchist, and that another third identified as anarchistic in some way. More generally, Bray notes that it "was nearly impossible to describe one's politics in terms of the movement without situating them in relation to anarchism"; see Mark Bray, Translating Anarchy: The Anarchism of Occupy Wall Street *(Winchester, UK: Zero Books, 2013), 42.*

The Principles of Solidarity of Occupy Wall Street

On September 17, 2011, people from all across the United States of America and the world came to protest the blatant injustices of our times perpetuated by the economic and political elites. On the 17th we as individuals rose up against political disenfranchisement and social and economic injustice. We spoke out, resisted, and successfully occupied Wall Street. Today, we proudly remain in Liberty Square constituting ourselves as autonomous political beings engaged in non-violent civil disobedience and building solidarity based on mutual respect, acceptance, and love. It is from these reclaimed grounds that we say to all Americans and to the world, Enough! How many crises does it take? We are the 99% and we have moved to reclaim our mortgaged future. Through a direct democratic process, we have come together as individuals and crafted these principles of solidarity, which are points of unity that include but are not limited to:

- Engaging in direct and transparent participatory democracy;
- Exercising personal and collective responsibility;
- Recognizing individuals' inherent privilege and the influence it has on all interactions;
- Empowering one another against all forms of oppression;
- Redefining how labor is valued;
- The sanctity of individual privacy;
- The belief that education is human right; and
- Making technologies, knowledge, and culture open to all to freely access, create, modify, and distribute. (amendment passed by consensus 2/9/2012)

We are daring to imagine a new socio-political and economic alternative that offers greater possibility of equality. We are consolidating the other proposed principles of solidarity, after which demands will follow.

d. Declaration of the Occupation of New York City, accepted by the NYC General Assembly on September 29, 2011

As we gather together in solidarity to express a feeling of mass injustice, we must not lose sight of what brought us together. We write so that all people who feel wronged by the corporate forces of the world can know that we are your allies.

As one people, united, we acknowledge the reality: that the future of the human race requires the cooperation of its members; that our system must protect our rights, and upon corruption of that system, it is up to the individuals to protect their own rights, and those of their neighbors; that a democratic government derives its just power from the people, but corporations do not seek consent to extract wealth from the people and the Earth; and that no true democracy is attainable when the process is determined by economic power. We come to you at a time when corporations, which place profit over people, self-interest over justice, and oppression over equality, run our governments. We have peaceably assembled here, as is our right, to let these facts be known.

- They have taken our houses through an illegal foreclosure process, despite not having the original mortgage.
- They have taken bailouts from taxpayers with impunity, and continue to give Executives exorbitant bonuses.
- They have perpetuated inequality and discrimination in the workplace based on age, the color of one's skin, sex, gender identity and sexual orientation.
- They have poisoned the food supply through negligence, and undermined the farming system through monopolization.
- They have profited off of the torture, confinement, and cruel treatment of countless animals, and actively hide these practices.
- They have continuously sought to strip employees of the right to negotiate for better pay and safer working conditions.
- They have held students hostage with tens of thousands of dollars of debt on education, which is itself a human right.
- They have consistently outsourced labor and used that outsourcing as leverage to cut workers' healthcare and pay.
- They have influenced the courts to achieve the same rights as people, with none of the culpability or responsibility.
- They have spent millions of dollars on legal teams that look for ways to get them out of contracts in regard to health insurance.

- They have sold our privacy as a commodity.
- They have used the military and police force to prevent freedom of the press.
- They have deliberately declined to recall faulty products endangering lives in pursuit of profit.
- They determine economic policy, despite the catastrophic failures their policies have produced and continue to produce.
- They have donated large sums of money to politicians, who are responsible for regulating them.
- They continue to block alternate forms of energy to keep us dependent on oil.
- They continue to block generic forms of medicine that could save people's lives or provide relief in order to protect investments that have already turned a substantial profit.
- They have purposely covered up oil spills, accidents, faulty bookkeeping, and inactive ingredients in pursuit of profit.
- They purposefully keep people misinformed and fearful through their control of the media.
- They have accepted private contracts to murder prisoners even when presented with serious doubts about their guilt.
- They have perpetuated colonialism at home and abroad.
- They have participated in the torture and murder of innocent civilians overseas.
- They continue to create weapons of mass destruction in order to receive government contracts.*

To the people of the world, We, the New York City General Assembly occupying Wall Street in Liberty Square, urge you to assert your power. Exercise your right to peaceably assemble; occupy public space; create a process to address the problems we face, and generate solutions accessible to everyone. To all communities that take action and form groups in the spirit of direct democracy, we offer support, documentation, and all of the resources at our disposal. Join us and make your voices heard!

*These grievances are not all-inclusive.

e. Principles of Democratic Confederalism

Extracted from Abdullah Ocalan, Democratic Confederalism, *trans. International Initiative (London: Transmedia Publishing, 2015), 33–34. Abdullah Ocalan is the imprisoned leader of the Kurdish Workers' Party (PKK). His vision of democratic confederalism, strongly influenced by the work of Murray Bookchin, has shaped the experiment in decentralised non-state government in Rojava. In 2016, Kurdish, Arab, Syriac-Assyrian and Turkmen groups reconstituted themselves as an autonomous administration in North and East Syria, implementing Ocalan's principles of local governance, direct democracy and gender equality; see Debbie Bookchin, "How My Father's Ideas Helped the Kurds Create a New Democracy",* New York Review, *June 15, 2018.*

1 The right of self-determination of the peoples includes the right to a state of their own. However, the foundation of a state does not increase the freedom of a people. The system of the United Nations that is based on nation-states has remained inefficient. Meanwhile, nation-states have become serious obstacles for any social development. Democratic confederalism is the contrasting paradigm of the oppressed people.

2 Democratic confederalism is a non-state social paradigm. It is not controlled by a state. At the same time, democratic confederalism is the cultural organizational blueprint of a democratic nation.

3 Democratic confederalism is based on grass-roots participation. Its decision-making processes lie with the communities. Higher levels only serve the coordination and implementation of the will of the communities that send their delegates to the general assemblies. For limited

space of time they are both mouthpiece and executive institutions. However, the basic power of decision rests with the local grass-roots institutions.

4   In the Middle East, democracy cannot be imposed by the capitalist system and its imperial powers which only damage democracy. The propagation of grass-roots democracy is elementary. It is the only approach that can cope with diverse ethnical groups, religions, and class differences. It also goes together well with the traditional confederate structure of the society.

5   Democratic confederalism in Kurdistan is an anti-nationalist movement as well. It aims at realizing the right of self-defence of the peoples by the advancement of democracy in all parts of Kurdistan without questioning the existing political borders. Its goal is not the foundation of a Kurdish nation state. The movement intends to establish federal structures in Iran, Turkey, Syria, and Iraq that are open for all Kurds and at the same time form an umbrella confederation for all four parts of Kurdistan.

2. Institutions

How should groups check or balance power within them? This is a key constitutional question. The following sources set out the principles that should underpin the institutional organisation and sub-division of larger organisations.

a. Organogram of the Wales, Ireland, England and Scotland Regional Administration of the Industrial Workers of the World (IWW)

As the following chart demonstrates, the IWW's structure places the individual member and the General Members Branch at the heart of union organising. Branches delegate members to act as officers or as branch delegates to the regional Delegate Executive Council (DEC). Branch delegates have oversight and responsibility for the accountability of the Union's activities and committees, between conferences. Union officers have no voting rights at the DEC level; only Delegates can vote, thereby expressing the will of the general membership.

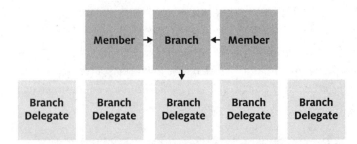

Member → Branch ← Member

Branch Delegate | Branch Delegate | Branch Delegate | Branch Delegate | Branch Delegate

Branch Delegates vote, representing their branches' views

Delegate Executive Council

Policy and decision-making, instruction and scrutiny of IWW officers, departments and committee

Regional Officers do not vote, but report on the work done by departments and committees

Departments, Committees, Officers

Admin Department

Regional Secretary

Regional Treasurer

Membership Officer

Legal Officer

International Officer

International Committee

IT Committee

Research and Survey Committee

Organising Department

Org Dept Chair

Area Organisers

General Organisers

Women's Officer

LGBTQIA+ Officer

BAME Officer

Access Officer

Environment Committee

Equalities Committee

Industrial Networks

Prisoner Solidarity Network

Training Committee

Communications Department

Comms Officer

Branch Comms Officers

Literature Committee

Merchandise Committee

b. To All the Peasants and Workers of the Ukraine: The Military Revolutionary Council and Command Staff of the Revolutionary Insurgent Army of the Ukraine (Makhnovists), January 7, 1920

The Makhnovists were a guerrilla army organised by Nestor Makhno which promoted anarchism in the Ukraine between 1918–1921. This declaration is reprinted from Paul Avrich, ed., The Anarchists in the Russian Revolution *(London: Thames and Hudson, 1973), 133–35.*

To be transmitted by telegraph, telephone, or post to all villages, townships, districts, and provinces of the Ukraine. To be read in village assemblies, factories, and workshops.

Brother toilers! The Revolutionary, Insurgent Army of the Ukraine (Makhnovists) was called into being as a protest against the oppression of workers and peasants by the bourgeois-landlord authorities on one side and the Bolshevik-Communist dictatorship on the other. Setting itself the goal to fight for the complete liberation of the toilers of the Ukraine from the yoke of this or that power and to create a *true soviet socialist order*, the Insurgent Army of Makhnovists has fought persistently on several fronts to achieve these objectives and at the present time to finish the struggle against Denikin's army, liberating district after district from every coercive power and every coercive organisation.

Many peasants and workers have raised the question: What will there be now? What is to be done? How shall we respond to the decrees of the evicted authorities? etc. To all such questions the final answer will be given by the All-Ukrainian Workers' and Peasants' Congress, which must meet at once, as soon as the workers and peasants are able to attend it. This congress will discuss and decide all urgent questions concerning worker and peasant life.

In view of the fact that such a congress will soon be convened, the Insurgent Army of Makhnovists deems it necessary to issue the following declaration concerning the questions of worker and peasant life:

1 All decrees of the Denikin (Voluntary) Army are hereby abolished. Those decrees of the Communist authorities which conflict with the interests of the peasants and workers are likewise abolished.
   Note: In this connection, which of the decrees of the Communist authorities are harmful to the toilers must be decided by the toilers themselves in their village assemblies and in the factories and shops.

2 The land of the gentry, the church and other enemies of the toilers with all its livestock and equipment must be transferred to the peasants, who will live on it only by their own labour. The transfer will take place in organised manner, according to the decisions of peasant assemblies, which must take into account not only their own local interests but also common interests of the whole oppressed labouring peasantry.

3 The factories, workshops, mines, and other means of production are to become the possession of the working class as a whole, which through its trade unions will take all enterprises in its own hands, resume production, and strive to link together the industry of the whole country in a single united organisation.

4 It is proposed that all organisations of workers and peasants begin to create free workers' and peasants' soviets. These soviets must consist only of toilers engaged in some form of labour that is necessary for the national economy. Representatives of political organisations have no place in workers' and peasants' soviets, for their participation will transform the latter into soviets of party deputies, which can only bring about the demise of the soviet order.

5   The existence of Chekas, party committees or similar coercive, authoritarian, and disciplinarian institutions is impermissible among peasants and workers.

6   Freedom of speech, press, assembly, trade unions and the like is an inalienable right of every worker, and any limitation of this right represents a counter-revolutionary act.

7   State militias, police and armies are hereby abolished. In their place people will organise their own self-defence units. Self-defence must be organised only by workers and peasants.

8   The workers' and peasants' soviets, the self-defence units of the workers and peasants, and the individual peasant and worker must not allow any counter-revolutionary manifestations by the *bourgeoisie* or military officers. Nor must they allow the emergence of banditry. Anyone convicted of counter-revolutionary acts or of banditry will be shot on the spot.

9   Soviet and Ukrainian money must be accepted along with all other kinds of money. Violators of this rule will be subject to revolutionary punishment.

10   The exchange of goods and products, until taken over by workers' and peasants' organisations, will remain free. But at the same time it is proposed that the exchange of products take place for the most part *between toilers*.

11   All individuals who attempt to hinder the distribution of this declaration will be regarded as counter-revolutionaries.

3. Decision-Making Procedures

Anarchist and anarchistic organisations use different types of democratic decision-making depending on the types of decisions that need to be made. Because each individual is considered relatively sovereign, consensus is the norm in most anarchist organisations. Voting is often seen as a sign of failure, because a minority will always be excluded. For this reason supermajorities are often favoured over simple majorities. How decisions are made is not separate from deciding which issues need a decision. How the organisation is structured will shape what sorts of decisions it is possible to make, when and where.

a. Radical Routes Model General Rules for New Cooperatives

Radical Routes is a secondary cooperative, or a federal body, that brings together and supports almost two dozen UK anarchist housing and worker cooperatives. All of the houses and workplaces are fully mutualised, meaning no one can profit individually or sell the property, and all profits are shared equally among members and/or donated to Radical Routes to support the running and expansion of the federation. The extracts below are taken from their Model Rules.

Governance of the Co-operative shall take place by General Meeting only. There shall be no power under these Rules to establish a committee of management. A general meeting shall have the power to appoint, replace and remove individuals, members or groups of members delegated to exercise certain powers on behalf of the Co-operative.

a) General meetings of the Co-operative should be attended by all members; and all members present shall be entitled to speak, participate in decision making and, where needed, vote.

b) Each member shall be given at least seven clear days' notice of the time and place of each general meeting and of the issues upon which decisions are to be taken. Notification will be deemed to have taken place if it was done through:

    i. email or telephone call from another member of the Co-operative, including time and place of the meeting and the issues to be raised.

    ii. circulation of minutes of the previous General Meeting in which the date of the next meeting and any relevant issues to be discussed were noted.

    iii. an agenda, including time, date and place, being displayed on an official noticeboard seven days in advance.

    iv. a letter.

Except when all the members, and lessees with voting rights, of the Cooperative are present and there is unanimous agreement among them, in which case they are empowered to constitute a general meeting at that point in time or at a specified time and place. This can include live participation via telephone and/or internet.

c) A General Meeting shall be called by the Secretary in accordance with the Co-operative's rules or policies, or by not less than three members or one-tenth of the members of the Co-operative, whichever is the greater.

d) If no General Meeting has occurred within a three-month period any member shall be empowered to call such a meeting.

e) Special General Meetings of the Co-operative shall be conducted in the same manner as general meetings, except that they shall require twenty-eight clear days' notice to be given...

Decision-Making Processes

a) The decision-making process in the Co-operative in any meeting constituted under Rules 13 (General Meetings) and 14 (Quorum and Decision Making Powers), shall primarily be carried out using consensus decision-making, following an appropriate method as set out by a previous decision at a General Meeting, or as chosen by the members present.

 i. Any decision reached by consensus shall be considered to have been passed as if by vote.

 ii. Any consensus decision-making process shall include the selection of a facilitator who shall for all other purposes have the power of a chair.

b) Any general meeting may revert to the use of voting in order to decide an issue, provided the motion to go to voting is supported by no fewer than one third of those present, or two members, whichever is the greater. Where a motion to go to vote is carried, a chairperson shall be selected to ensure an orderly process of voting takes place. Any vote relating to matters governed by or change of these Rules, shall be held over until the next general meeting to allow members not in attendance to be present, or to provide a proxy vote in writing.

c) When a vote takes place, every member present in person at a general meeting shall have one vote. Except where otherwise specified in these Rules, resolutions shall be decided upon by a majority vote of members present and voting. Votes shall be taken openly, unless, before a motion is put to the vote, a secret ballot is demanded by not fewer than one sixth of the members present. Voting shall be conducted under the direction of the chairperson in accordance with any procedures agreed by the Co-operative. A motion on which voting is tied shall be deemed to have fallen.

d) A general meeting shall take into account submissions from a member who cannot make the meeting, but such submissions shall not count towards quoracy unless they specifically address an agenda item that has been circulated in advance.

e) Where the Co-operative has only three members and Rule 14(e) imposes a unanimous decision...

b. Heartwood Cohousing Decision Making and Meetings Agreement

Heartwood is a neighbourhood co-housing project in Colorado, founded in 2000. It is not explicitly anarchist but it models a non-hierarchical approach to consensus decision-making that resonates with horizontal and anarchist organisations. Note how this lengthy set of instructions combines decision making, institutions, rules and constitutive statements about who the group is and what they stand for.

All decisions are made by a consensus of members whether in Community Meetings, Team Meetings, or by Posted Decision. The only exceptions are when we elect to use an alternative decision-making method (see "Alternative Method Vote" below) or a Fallback Resolution Process (see "Fallback Resolution Process" below).

The result of a community decision is an agreement. Members are required to follow agreements. The result of a team decision is a guideline. Members are strongly encouraged to follow guidelines.

All decisions remain in force until they are replaced by another decision. A team may reconsider any of their previous decisions at any time. A community decision previously made is reconsidered only if:

a) A majority of voting member households wants to reconsider the decision. Requests for reconsideration of a decision must be in writing (petition, email, etc.).

b) The Steering Team decides that there is significant cause to reconsider the decision.

c) A team or task force decides that there is significant cause to reconsider a decision within their area of responsibility. For decisions that directly impact the children, children's input is sought.

Quorum

A quorum is not necessary for consensus decisions because of the ability of absentee members to vote. (See "Absentee Member Voting" below.) A quorum is, however, necessary to take an Alternative Method Vote. A quorum is established by the presence of at least one voting member from 51 percent of all voting member households.

Posted Decisions

Community decisions may be made using the Posted Decision method. A Posted Decision is made using the following steps:

- Topic Guide posts a proposal to a posting place designated by the Steering Team.
- (The designated posting place may be electronic or physical and must be easily accessible and well known. It is used for Posted Decisions and Community and Team meeting agendas and minutes.)
  - The proposal specifically includes:
    - Name of Topic.
    - Name of Topic Guide.
    - Posting Date.
    - Input Deadline Date (10 days after Posting Date).
    - Background information.
    - Proposal.

- All voting members have until the Input Deadline Date to provide input in writing to the designated posting place.
- Note: Voting members must be specific when giving input as to whether the input is a comment (blue card), a

concern not needing to be addressed (orange card), or a concern that does need to be addressed (red card).

- If a voting member raises a red card concern, they work with the Topic Guide to resolve their concern, which could lead to modifying the proposal. A modified proposal is reposted using the same guidelines as though it were a new proposal.

- Note: The Topic Guide may choose for any reason to withdraw the proposal and have it considered at a Community Meeting rather than as a Posted Decision.

- If no red card concerns are raised (or if they are raised and later withdrawn) before the Input Deadline Date AND the Topic Guide has posted a follow up stating whether or not the proposal passed, the proposal becomes a decision. The Topic Guide is also expected to post a follow up if the proposal has not passed.

Alternative Method Vote

When the community feels that some alternative decision-making method is more appropriate than consensus, we may choose an alternative decision-making method by taking an Alternative Method Vote (applies only to community, not team, decisions). To pass, the Alternative Method Vote requires a 75 percent vote of the voting member households present (one vote per voting member household). The alternative method of decision making may employ voting on a per person basis, a per household basis, or in whatever manner the community decides during the Alternative Method Vote . . .

Absentee Member Voting

Only members who are present at a meeting may vote (i.e., no voting by proxy), except as allowed by the following Absentee Member Voting procedure (applies only to community, not team, decisions). The Absentee Member Voting option cannot be exercised in any decisions involving an Alternative Method Vote.

- At least two days before the Community Meeting, an Absentee Member choosing to block a proposal to be decided upon must inform the facilitator by some means of confirmed communication. (That is, the facilitator must confirm with the Absentee Member that they have been informed of the Absentee Member's choice to block the proposal.)
- If an Absentee Member chooses to affirm a proposal, they may do so by sending word to the meeting via any representative to the meeting they choose.

Types of Meetings
Community
Purpose: To conduct the normal business of the community where full community participation is appropriate.
Authority to Call Meeting: Steering team—on an as needed basis.
Decisions Made: Community decisions.
Essential Roles:

- Facilitator to guide the discussion and/or decision making to accomplish the stated agenda purpose(s) while ensuring that Ground Rules are followed.
- Keeper of the Heart to attend to the participants' emotional well-being.
- Topic Guide to present a topic being considered (as part of their overall responsibility to oversee and guide the progress of a topic all the way through to its resolution).
- Recorder to keep and post minutes (and revise if necessary).

Participation:

- Observer: Anyone is welcome to come and observe without participating. Observers are allowed to participate only during the opening and closing of the meeting—not while topics are being addressed. Exceptions to this:

- Input solicited from an expert on the topic being considered.
- All attendees are welcome to participate in discussions and practice during training and education type meetings.

- Voting Member: A member becomes a voting member after they have attended 3 Community Meetings within six months. (Community Meetings attended before becoming a member do count towards this requirement.) A voting member is entitled to fully participate in Community Meetings, Team Meetings, and the Posted Decision process. (That is, they observe for three meetings and then participate at the fourth.)

Meeting of the Hearts
Purpose: To provide an opportunity for open sharing of values and feelings and for the community to work on interpersonal relations and group process thereby creating a greater level of tolerance, respect, empathy, and understanding amongst members, all of which will help reduce potential conflicts.
Authority to Call Meeting: Process and Communication team.
Meetings of the Heart are held at least once every two months.
Decisions Made: None.
Essential Roles: None.
Participation: Anyone.

Team
Purpose: To conduct the normal business of the community which has been delegated to a team.
Authority to Call Meeting: Team members—on an as needed basis.
Decisions Made: Team decisions.
Essential Roles: Facilitator to guide the discussion and/or decision making to accomplish the stated agenda purpose(s). Recorder to keep and post minutes.

Participation: Observers and Voting Members only (see "Community Meetings" section above).

Sharing Circle

Purpose: To provide an opportunity for open sharing of values and feelings around a particular topic—not for discussing ideas or problem solving.

Authority to Call Meeting: Anyone (person calling meeting must define the topic and purpose of the meeting when they call it and at the beginning of the meeting).

Decisions Made: None.

Essential Roles: Person who called the meeting to facilitate as needed.

Participation: Anyone.

Discussion Circle

Purpose: To provide an opportunity for open discussion of ideas or problem solving around a particular topic.

Authority to Call Meeting: Anyone (person calling meeting must define the topic and purpose of the meeting when they call it and at the beginning of the meeting).

Decisions Made: None.

Essential Roles: Person who called the meeting to facilitate as needed. Recorder to keep and post minutes.

Participation: Anyone.

Retreat

Purpose: To reconsider the "Big Picture" topics (where we're at as a community, the nature of the community, and our Core agreements) and to work on core community skills (communication, conflict resolution, etc.).

Authority to Call Meeting: Steering or Process and Communication team. Retreats are held annually.

Decisions Made: None, unless previously authorized by community.

Essential Roles: Facilitator to guide the process to accomplish the stated agenda purpose(s).

Participation: Members only. The team calling the retreat may grant exceptions for outside facilitators and other guests under special circumstances.

Special

Purpose: To handle any special business that the Steering Team feels warrants a special meeting.

Authority to Call Meeting: Steering team—on an as needed basis.

Decisions Made: None, unless previously authorized by community.

Essential Roles: Determined by the Steering team.

Participation: Determined by the Steering team.

Community and Team Meetings Ground Rules

- Address each other with compassion.
- Silence means agreement.
- One person speaks at a time.
- No personal attacks.
- Share the air time.

Community and Team Meetings Content

Posting the Agenda

Agenda must be posted on the designated posting place at least four days before the meeting (provides members with the information needed to decide whether or not to attend meeting and allows for Absentee Voting at Community Meetings).

Each Agenda item will include:

- Purpose (what is to be accomplished).
- Topic Guide.
- Clearly stated topic.
- Possibly a Proposal.

Opening the Meeting

Begin on time.

Review and get agreement on meeting Agenda and Purpose(s).

Review Ground Rules.

Working with Topics and Making Decisions

All voting members are given an opportunity to comment and/
or express concerns on a topic. Intellectual and emotional
input are both welcome. Decisions are to be made from the
community's perspective. A voting member may choose to
red card or Stand in the Way of a decision when s/he believes
that the decision would be seriously wrong for the group, not
because s/he personally disagrees with it. A voting member
may also choose to Stand Aside in making a decision, which
means that s/he personally doesn't agree with the decision
but doesn't see it as contrary to the stated values of the
community.

Major concerns with a proposal are concerns that a voting
member considers significant enough to warrant having the
community or team work to resolve. A major concern is indi-
cated by a red card that stops the process in a straw poll or
consensus "vote." Major concerns are recorded, indicating who
has concerns and what the concerns are. Each major concern
is discussed until the person(s) holding the concern feels that
the concern has been satisfactorily addressed, except in the
case of a Fallback Resolution Process (see "Fallback Resolution
Process" below).

Because a red card stops the process until it is resolved, it
is important to remember that a red card presents an opportunity to explore and understand more fully any issues with
a proposal. How the community works with a red card has
the potential to increase cooperation and connection within
the group. Both the red card holder and the community must
explore the red card concern with full seriousness and respect,
in a spirit of mutuality.

Proposals at Community Meetings may not be modified and consensed at the same meeting, however, because of the need to allow for Absentee Voting (doesn't apply to Team Meetings). A consensus decision is made once there are no major unresolved concerns remaining.

Fallback Resolution Process

If one or more members red cards a proposal, the red card holder(s) is responsible for organizing meetings with the Topic Guide(s) who presented the proposal or their appointed representatives, and any other interested members in a series of solution-oriented, consensus-building meetings. The purpose of the meetings is to work through the concerns and mutually agree on a revised proposal that addresses the same problem as the original blocked proposal. These meetings must take place within two months. It is recommended that four meetings are held, if needed, to find resolution and create a revised proposal.

If a revised proposal is created within two months of the red card, the revised proposal is brought to the community for consideration as a new proposal.

If resolution cannot be achieved and no revised proposal is created within two months of the red card, the original blocked proposal is brought to the next available Community Meeting for a Fallback Supermajority Vote. The original blocked proposal passes, resulting in a community decision, if a supermajority of 80% of the members present at the Community Meeting vote for the proposal.

The two-month clock for the Fallback Resolution Process starts running in the case of any of the following:

1 Community Meeting ends with an unresolved red card concern in a straw poll.
2 Community Meeting ends with an unresolved red card concern in a consensus vote.

3 Red card is posted in a posted decision proposal.

Closing the Meeting

End on time, or agree to extend.

Critique the meeting. (What went well? What could we do differently?)

Communication on Email Chat

Members are responsible for information and decisions posted on the Heartwood email chat. Members posting information on the chat may assume that all Members will become aware of it.

4. Rules and Rule-Making

The spoken or written rules of an organisation are only part of what helps it function. Often the unspoken rules and habits can be oppressive, especially if you are not aware of them, or are not a member of the cliquey groups that establish them. Making rules visible and being conscious of them, and of how to change them, is vital to avoid the habitual or systematic domination of one group by another. Patriarchy is one such habitual structure of power, but race and class are others. We have used examples of two attempts to address gender-based violence because they show that it is possible to address this in a non-dominating way within anarchist groups.

a. Solidarity Federation (SolFed) UK: Statement about Sexual Assault within the Anarchist/Activist Community (Monday, May 25, 2012)

Solidarity Federation (SolFed) was founded in 1994 as a section of the International Workers' Federation. Members organised in "locals" are networked across England, Ireland, Scotland and Wales. It is a non-hierarchical, anti-authoritarian solidarity promoting community and worker's self-management by direct action. The statement was posted online on May 25, 2012.

This statement comes from recent discussions within South London and North London Solidarity Federation locals, and in response to a recent case of sexual assault which took place in the wider activist community. Following the actions taken by North London, South London and Brighton Solidarity Federation locals, this statement was written by the South London Gender Working Group.

We want to state clearly a number of things.

We believe that in the event of sexual assault it is necessary to take action, and that it is appropriate to look towards processes of community accountability. In exploring how to deal with such situations, we have looked at the experiences of other activist and political communities, and the literature that has stemmed from these. We strongly support other groups who have initiated these processes; these enact a sense of responsibility and care we should have for and with each other.

It is entirely appropriate to exclude the perpetrator from spaces which the survivor may wish to be in, so as to avoid creating a platform for the particular abusive relationship to continue. It is clear that for many people, activism and politics are the environments in which they seek to form abusive relationships; therefore we exclude them from our spaces and events. In light of this, excluding a perpetrator from our events and meetings is a likely initial response that we will make to an account of abuse, and we defend our decision to do so.

In one particular recent case, a number of SolFed locals and members have come under attack for taking such a stance. It is our understanding that within similar situations it is fairly common for the survivor who calls someone out, or those who support them, to come under attack. It is not uncommon that this is in the form of endless questions around language and the very foundations of accountability processes.

In this statement we want to express our continued commitment to processes of community accountability. While we believe that all processes within a political community such as ours should be subjected to critique, we take seriously recent expressions of groups intent on disrupting any of these processes. We encourage those who have stated this as their intention to reconsider their position. This case of sexual assault comes out of a wider background of gendered violence, misogyny, sexism and patriarchy which are perpetuated within activist communities and often go unchallenged. As such, neither this individual case, nor our responses to it, can be seen in isolation.

At the same time we call for solidarity with all processes of community accountability. We invite the wider activist community to engage with the feminist tradition of these processes. It is of huge importance for political communities to maintain the safety of the spaces they create, and address questions of privilege.

b. Occupy London Online Safer Spaces Policy

The policy was introduced in December 2011 in response to complaints about the moderators of the livestream.

Open discussion is at the heart of Occupy London. The more people we can involve in our debates, the stronger and more representative the results will be.

Occupy London wants to operate and conduct our discussions in a safe space that is welcoming, engaging and supportive. In order to ensure this we have established some guidelines for participants. These have been agreed by the OccupyLSX General Assembly.

Please note that, as with all forms of direct democracy, this policy is a work in progress. Suggestions are welcome.

1   **Safer space**. Racism, as well as ageism, homophobia, sexism, transphobia, ableism or prejudice based on ethnicity, impairment, nationality, class, gender, gender presentation, language ability, asylum status or religious affiliation will not be tolerated.

2   **Respect**. Foster a spirit of mutual respect: Listen to the wisdom everyone brings to the group. Recognize that we try not to judge, put each other down or compete.

3   **Assumptions**. Avoid assuming the opinions and identifications of other participants. If in doubt, ask.

4   **Awareness**. Be aware of the language you use in discussion and how you relate to others. Be conscious that people may understand your words differently than you intended.

5   **Accessibility**. Try to communicate clearly and use plain language. Remember Occupy aims to be the movement

of the 99%, so be mindful of diverse backgrounds and perspectives.

6 **Criticism**. Constructive criticism and dissent are welcome, but should be focused on the issue not the person. Personal attacks and false and defamatory accusations will not be accepted.

7 **Spam**. Repeat posting of the same off-topic posts and spamming of links that have nothing to do with the subject will be banned. This may also apply to people or organisations who frequently post external links or propaganda without adding to the quality of the discussion online. Memberships created solely for these purposes will be banned.

8 **Autonomy and self-promotion**. Any statement or declaration not released through the General Assembly and made public online should be considered independent of Occupy London. Self-promotional links to one's own blog, video channel, product, business, etc., even if related to Occupy, are limited to one's own forum signature and user profile.

9 **On topic**. If something is posted which is unrelated to the original topic then it may be removed, or moved to a relevant thread by the moderators, in order to keep the thread on track. Before posting, please ask yourself if you're making a contribution to the discussion and if you are posting in the right thread.

10 **Banning**. Posts that do not respect the above guidelines will be removed immediately. Users who repeatedly ignore the above guidelines will be informed that if they continue, they will be banned. Users who have been notified but continue to ignore the guidelines, will be banned. According to the situation a ban can be temporary or indefinite.

11 **Moderation**. Moderators help enforce these guidelines. The point of moderation is not to limit discussion, or to

promote or suppress points of view. The goal of moderation is to keep the forums enjoyable and free from problems that detract from the aim of the media platforms and the experiences of users. Should a moderator abuse her/his position, the other moderators can collectively decide to withdraw moderator status.

12 **Responsibility**. The bad behaviour of one member is not an excuse for another to not respect this safer space policy. These guidelines are a collective responsibility: everyone is personally responsible for their own behaviour. The moderators cannot read all posts so they rely on members to report problems that they encounter.

Worksheets to Help You Put It All into Practice

The following worksheets take some of the tricky problems we have highlighted in this book and provide suggestions for how to chart a course through them. They were co-designed with Jed Picksley, who has used *Anarchic Agreements* to support numerous organisations across the UK. The structure of the worksheets is also inspired by the Viable Systems Model (VSM) of cybernetic organisation. For an excellent primer on VSM, check out Jon Walker's *The Viable Systems Model: A Guide for Co-operatives and Federations*. Walker's guide was originally written in 1998, with a third edition published in 2020. The guide provides in-depth advice on using the model in groups and federations. Walker was once a member of Suma and other workers' cooperatives and applied the VSM, originally developed by Stafford Beer, to non-hierarchical organisation. Walker also used the VSM in work he did with Radical Routes. We think his approach aligns closely with our intentions for this book.

1. What's the purpose?

Starting out	Reviewing and introducing new people	Strength tests
a. Has everyone discussed the group's aims and principles?	e. Can you easily explain the aims and principles to new members?	g. How well are the group's aims and principles being met in practice?
b. How much do you want to rely on shared understanding or trust?	f. Can you say what you each value about the group?	h. How are you managing differences in organisational practice?
c. Are there groups or individuals you want to work with or will never work with?		i. What if someone or a group wants to leave?
d. Who is outside the group but is still impacted by your activities?		

- What is the group for?
- What is your focus?
- What are the boundaries of your activities?
- Who are you interacting with?

1a. From memory, collectively define the groups aims and principles.

1b. Make suggestions about what your expectations of each other could be.

1c. List groups you could work with or would never work with.

1d. Visually illustrate the group's key concerns and how they affect other groups or sub-groups.

1e. Try summarising what holds the group together in less than fifty words, and in under a minute!

1f. Each of you write down two things you value about the group or coalition. Discuss any differences.

1g. Ask your neighbours/local institutions if they have noticed your group and what they think it stands for!

1h. List which roles have a job description and which don't yet.

1i. Reflect on times when people have left. Reflect on whether it was a failure of the group or natural growth.

2. What's in place?

Starting out	Reviewing and introducing new people	Strength tests
a. What do you need to organise, run or control collectively?	c. How do you provide access to shared papers?	f. How do you enable cooperation through communication?
b. Who should meet and how often?	d. Can you explain to each other how the group works?	g. Is control of tools and resources accountable and transparent?
	e. Do you need to explain your current practices to new members?	

- Agreements on procedures or responsibilities?
- Nothing?
- Bundles of notes and papers in a box file?
- Are you having meetings?

2a. Map the institution—list the different areas and functions that constitute the group or coalition and/or decide which roles and responsibilities sit with specific individuals, and which are shared between the group(s).

2b. Check who in the group is storing documents that could put anyone at risk and how (data protection).

2c. Make both "procedure" agreements and "policy" agreements and/or compile the group's annual calendar of events, if it doesn't exist yet.

2d. Explain why you do or don't need a rota for different tasks.

2e. Consider developing an online collaborative page, like Loomio and/or discuss what it would take to make your aims and principles an outward facing publication?

2f. Check that database access is up to date, and that passwords are held securely and/or identify an item and organise a treasure hunt in your own filing system to find it!

3. What's the problem?

Starting out	Reviewing and introducing new people	Strength tests
a. What sort of relationships do you want to cultivate in your group?	d. Are you managing to reach agreements consensually?	g. What are you doing to build trust?
b. What are members' expectations?	e. Are new members able to learn how to take part in decision-making?	h. Do you need to set up a conflict resolution process for your group?
c. How will you run meetings, make decisions and record information?	f. Do you need mechanisms to help members raise objections or make proposals?	i. Do you need a facilitator?
		j. Do you need a policy or process for resolving disagreements between different groups?

- Conflict?
- Communication breakdown?
- Exhaustion?
- Lack of clarity?
- Apathy?
- Habits?

3a. Think about how personal or professional you want your group or coalition to be.

3b. Rank what you care most about: e.g., solidarity, recognition, reward or learning.

3c. Undertake a skills audit for your meetings, group or coalition.

3d. Decide which issues need consensus and which will get by on a supermajority.

3e. Draw a diagram of how decisions are made at the lowest appropriate level or use tea breaks as times to chat about the process of the meeting itself.

3f. Create a five-point guide to making proposals for an agenda that any member can use.

3g. Invite dissent and disagreement in "chat" at online meetings or in person.

3h. Look for existing examples of conflict resolution processes or peace-making procedures.

3i. Find a free facilitation training online: www.seedsfor change.org/resources.

3j. Find volunteers from within or outside the group/coalition to facilitate a meeting or help manage problems.

4. What's the plan?

Starting out	Reviewing and introducing new people	Strength tests
a. How will you evaluate the activities you do as a group?	d. Are you able to see whether or not things you've done have been successful?	i. Can you identify strengths and weaknesses in your current practice?
b. How will you plan activities so that they can be realistically achievable over time?	e. Can any tasks be delegated to individuals or sub-groups?	j. Are you able to track progress and have a general overview of different group activities?
c. How will you enable change or review?	f. Do you need to pool or share resources?	k. Is the group able to stay together and focus on its aims and principles as things change?
	g. Are there any things that you need to change?	
	h. Can you agree on a process for review?	

- Are activities in line with aims and principles?
- Are goals being achieved?
- Are you looking at changes outside the group that could have an impact on what you do?
- Are you planning ahead?

4a. Map what people in the group or coalition do in addition to the established aims and principles.

4b. Give everyone a chance to talk about the demands on their time, mobility and resources and say how they think they can contribute best to group activities.

4c. Agree on specific trigger points (like new people joining) then work on a process that would allow maximum reasonable participation.

4d. Remind yourselves of the positive, everyday things you do, like functioning as a group!

4e. List the advantages and disadvantages of delegating some tasks to sub-groups or individuals.

4f. Set aside some time to think about the practicalities of sharing.

4g. Without apportioning blame, list your group's failures.

4h. Map what you want to review against a set of specific, agreed upon goals.

4i. Talk about what you mean by shared goals and about what's going well and what's not.

4j. Organise a shared workspace or diary to enable people to record their activities.

4k. Explore how your group's principles translate into practical responsibilities or expectations.

5. What can you change?

• How easy do you want it to be to change things?	a. **Day-to-day activities**
	b. **Strategy**
	c. **Principles**

5a. Write down what you regard as uncontentious and/or list activities and actions that can be carried out in the group's name by anyone without discussion and those that cannot.

5b. Decide which individuals and sub-groups have full autonomy to change things, and how often things should be revised and/or make it clear who the co-signatories are, who holds the officer positions, etc. and keep that record up to date.

5c. Establish the core aims and principles that generally can't be changed except at AGMs or similar meetings and/or brainstorm some types of decisions that would need the agreement of the whole group.

Further Reading

For a full archive of this project, please visit: www.anarchyrules.info.

Kinna, Ruth. *The Government of No One: The Theory and Practice of Anarchism*. London: Penguin, 2019.

Kinna, Ruth, Alex Prichard, and Thomas Swann. "Anarchy in the USA: Five Years On, the Legacy of Occupy Wall Street and What It Can Teach Us in the Age of Trump". *Conversation*, November 10, 2016.

———. "Iceland's Crowd-Sourced Constitution: Hope for Disillusioned Voters Everywhere". *Conversation*, October 28, 2016.

Moyes, Richard, Thomas Nash, and Article 36 (2011). "Global Coalitions: An Introduction to Working in International Civil Society Partnerships". Accessed March 14, 2022. http://www.globalcoalitions.org/.

Parker, Martin, Konstantin Stoborod, and Thomas Swann, eds. *Anarchism, Organization and Management: Critical Perspectives for Students*. London: Routledge, 2020.

Prichard, Alex. *Anarchism: A Very Short Introduction*. Oxford: Oxford University Press, 2022.

Seeds for Change. *A Consensus Handbook: Co-operative Decision-Making for Activists, Co-ops and Communities*. Accessed March 14, 2022. www.seedsforchange.org.uk/handbookweb.pdf.

———. *Effective Groups: A Guide to Successful Group Organising, from Starting Up Groups to Keeping Them Going*. Accessed March 14, 2022. www.seedsforchange.org.uk/effectivegroups.pdf.

About the Authors

Ruth Kinna teaches at Loughborough University, UK. She has published numerous books on anarchism, historical and contemporary, and is a contributor to *Mutual Aid: An Illuminated Factor of Evolution* (PM Press, 2021). She is also a coeditor of *Libertarian Socialism: Politics in Black and Red* (PM Press, 2017).

Alex Prichard teaches international relations at the University of Exeter, UK. He has published widely on the international political thought of Pierre-Joseph Proudhon, most recently editing and writing an introduction to a new translation of his 1861 work *War and Peace* (AK Press, 2022). He is also the author of the new edition of *Anarchism: A Very Short Introduction* (Oxford University Press, 2022).

Thomas Swann writes on anarchist politics and alternative organization. He is the author of *Anarchist Cybernetics: Control and Communication in Radical Politics* (Bristol University Press, 2020). He is also coeditor of *Anarchism, Organization and Management* (Taylor and Francis, 2020), a book that introduces anarchism to business school students.

Seeds for Change is a workers' co-op of experienced campaigners and cooperators. It offers training, facilitation, online resources, and other support for campaigns, community groups, and cooperatives. It also provides open-access resources on campaigning, facilitation, and workshops. Its members authored *A Consensus Handbook: Co-operative Decision-Making for Activists, Co-ops and Communities* (2013).

ABOUT PM PRESS

PM Press is an independent, radical publisher
of books and media to educate, entertain, and
inspire. Founded in 2007 by a small group of
people with decades of publishing, media, and
organizing experience, PM Press amplifies the
voices of radical authors, artists, and activists.
Our aim is to deliver bold political ideas and vital stories to all walks
of life and arm the dreamers to demand the impossible. We have sold
millions of copies of our books, most often one at a time, face to face.
We're old enough to know what we're doing and young enough to know
what's at stake. Join us to create a better world.

PM Press
PO Box 23912
Oakland, CA 94623
www.pmpress.org

PM Press in Europe
europe@pmpress.org
www.pmpress.org.uk

FRIENDS OF PM PRESS

These are indisputably momentous times—the
financial system is melting down globally and
the Empire is stumbling. Now more than ever
there is a vital need for radical ideas.

In the many years since its founding—and on
a mere shoestring—PM Press has risen to the formidable challenge
of publishing and distributing knowledge and entertainment for the
struggles ahead. With hundreds of releases to date, we have published
an impressive and stimulating array of literature, art, music, politics, and
culture. Using every available medium, we've succeeded in connecting
those hungry for ideas and information to those putting them into
practice.

Friends of PM allows you to directly help impact, amplify, and revitalize
the discourse and actions of radical writers, filmmakers, and artists. It
provides us with a stable foundation from which we can build upon our
early successes and provides a much-needed subsidy for the materials
that can't necessarily pay their own way. You can help make that
happen—and receive every new title automatically delivered to your
door once a month—by joining as a Friend of PM Press. And, we'll throw
in a free T-shirt when you sign up.

Here are your options:

• **$30 a month** Get all books and pamphlets plus 50% discount on all
  webstore purchases

• **$40 a month** Get all PM Press releases (including CDs and DVDs)
  plus 50% discount on all webstore purchases

• **$100 a month** Superstar—Everything plus PM merchandise, free
  downloads, and 50% discount on all webstore purchases

For those who can't afford $30 or more a month, we have **Sustainer
Rates** at $15, $10 and $5. Sustainers get a free PM Press T-shirt and a
50% discount on all purchases from our website.

Your Visa or Mastercard will be billed once a month, until you tell us to
stop. Or until our efforts succeed in bringing the revolution around. Or
the financial meltdown of Capital makes plastic redundant. Whichever
comes first.

Mutual Aid: An Illuminated Factor of Evolution

Peter Kropotkin
Illustrated by N.O. Bonzo with an
Introduction by David Graeber
& Andrej Grubačić, Foreword by
Ruth Kinna, Postscript by GATS,
and an Afterword by Allan Antliff

ISBN: 978-1-62963-874-4 (paperback)
        978-1-62963-875-1 (hardcover)
$20.00/$59.95   336 pages

One hundred years after his death, Peter Kropotkin is still one of
the most inspirational figures of the anarchist movement. It is often
forgotten that Kropotkin was also a world-renowned geographer whose
seminal critique of the hypothesis of competition promoted by social
Darwinism helped revolutionize modern evolutionary theory. An admirer
of Darwin, he used his observations of life in Siberia as the basis for his
1902 collection of essays *Mutual Aid: A Factor of Evolution*. Kropotkin
demonstrated that mutually beneficial cooperation and reciprocity—in
both individuals and as a species—plays a far more important role
in the animal kingdom and human societies than does individualized
competitive struggle. Kropotkin carefully crafted his theory making the
science accessible. His account of nature rejected Rousseau's romantic
depictions and ethical socialist ideas that cooperation was motivated
by the notion of "universal love." His understanding of the dynamics of
social evolution shows us the power of cooperation—whether it is bison
defending themselves against a predator or workers unionizing against
their boss. His message is clear: solidarity is strength!

Every page of this new edition of *Mutual Aid* has been beautifully
illustrated by one of anarchism's most celebrated current artists, N.O.
Bonzo. The reader will also enjoy original artwork by GATS and insightful
commentary by David Graeber, Ruth Kinna, Andrej Grubačić, and Allan
Antliff.

*"N.O. Bonzo has created a rare document, updating Kropotkin's anarchist
classic* Mutual Aid, *by intertwining compelling imagery with an updated
text. Filled with illustrious examples, their art gives the words and histories,
past and present, resonance for new generations to seed flowers of
cooperation to push through the concrete of resistance to show liberatory
possibilities for collective futures."*
—scott crow, author of *Black Flags and Windmills* and *Setting Sights*

Libertarian Socialism:
Politics in Black and Red

Edited by Alex Prichard, Ruth Kinna,
Saku Pinta, and David Berry

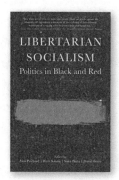

ISBN: 978-1-62963-390-9
$26.95   368 pages

The history of anarchist-Marxist relations is
usually told as a history of factionalism and
division. These essays, based on original
research and written especially for this collection, reveal some of the
enduring sores in the revolutionary socialist movement in order to
explore the important, too often neglected left-libertarian currents
that have thrived in revolutionary socialist movements. By turns, the
collection interrogates the theoretical boundaries between Marxism
and anarchism and the process of their formation, the overlaps and
creative tensions that shaped left-libertarian theory and practice, and
the stumbling blocks to movement cooperation. Bringing together
specialists working from a range of political perspectives, the book
charts a history of radical twentieth-century socialism, and opens
new vistas for research in the twenty-first. Contributors examine the
political and social thought of a number of leading socialists—Marx,
Morris, Sorel, Gramsci, Guérin, C.L.R. James, Hardt and Negri—and
key movements including the Situationist International, Socialisme
ou Barbarie and Council Communism. Analysis of activism in the UK,
Australasia, and the U.S. serves as the prism to discuss syndicalism,
carnival anarchism, and the anarchistic currents in the U.S. civil rights
movement.

Contributors include Paul Blackledge, Lewis H. Mates, Renzo Llorente,
Carl Levy, Christian Høgsbjerg, Andrew Cornell, Benoît Challand, Jean-
Christophe Angaut, Toby Boraman, and David Bates.

"Libertarian Socialism: Politics in Black and Red *is an invaluable*
contribution to historical scholarship and libertarian politics. The collection
of essays contained in the book has the great virtue of offering both
analytical perspectives on ideas, and historical perspectives on movements.
The contributions examine classical themes in anarchist politics such as
individual liberty, whilst also exploring more neglected thinkers and themes
from a libertarian standpoint, such as C.L.R. James and race. There can be
little doubt that the volume will be of major interest to historians, theorists,
students and activists."
—Darrow Schecter, reader in Italian, School of History, Art History and
Philosophy, University of Sussex

For All the People: Uncovering the Hidden History of Cooperation, Cooperative Movements, and Communalism in America, 2nd Edition

John Curl with an Introduction by Ishmael Reed

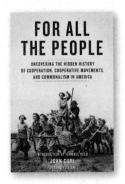

ISBN: 978-1-60486-582-0
$29.95   608 pages

Seeking to reclaim a history that has remained largely ignored by most historians, this dramatic and stirring account examines each of the definitive American cooperative movements for social change—farmer, union, consumer, and communalist—that have been all but erased from collective memory. Focusing far beyond one particular era, organization, leader, or form of cooperation, *For All the People* documents the multigenerational struggle of the American working people for social justice. While the economic system was in its formative years, generation after generation of American working people challenged it by organizing visionary social movements aimed at liberating themselves from what they called wage slavery. Workers substituted a system based on cooperative work and constructed parallel institutions that would supersede the institutions of the wage system.

With an expansive sweep and breathtaking detail, this scholarly yet eminently readable chronicle follows the American worker from the colonial workshop to the modern mass-assembly line, from the family farm to the corporate hierarchy, ultimately painting a vivid panorama of those who built the United States and those who will shape its future.

This second edition contains a new introduction by Ishmael Reed; a new author's preface discussing cooperatives in the Great Recession of 2008 and their future in the 21st century; and a new chapter on the role co-ops played in the Food Revolution of the 1970s.

"It is indeed inspiring, in the face of all the misguided praise of 'the market', to be reminded by John Curl's new book of the noble history of cooperative work in the United States."
—Howard Zinn, author of *A People's History of the United States*

Towards Collective Liberation: Anti-Racist Organizing, Feminist Praxis, and Movement Building Strategy

Chris Crass with an Introduction by Chris Dixon and Foreword by Roxanne Dunbar-Ortiz

ISBN: 978-1-60486-654-4
$20.00   320 pages

Towards Collective Liberation: Anti-Racist Organizing, Feminist Praxis, and Movement Building Strategy is for activists engaging with dynamic questions of how to create and support effective movements for visionary systemic change. Chris Crass's collection of essays and interviews presents us with powerful lessons for transformative organizing through offering a firsthand look at the challenges and the opportunities of anti-racist work in white communities, feminist work with men, and bringing women of color feminism into the heart of social movements. Drawing on two decades of personal activist experience and case studies of anti-racist social justice organizations, Crass insightfully explores ways of transforming divisions of race, class, and gender into catalysts for powerful vision, strategy, and movement building in the United States today.

"*In his writing and organizing, Chris Crass has been at the forefront of building the grassroots, multi-racial, feminist movements for justice we need.* Towards Collective Liberation *takes on questions of leadership, building democratic organizations, and movement strategy, on a very personal level that invites us all to experiment and practice the way we live our values while struggling for systemic change.*"
—Elizabeth 'Betita' Martinez, founder of the Institute for Multiracial Justice and author of *De Colores Means All of Us: Latina Views for a Multi-Colored Century*

"*Chris Crass goes into the grassroots to produce a political vision that will catalyze political change. These are words from the heart, overflowing onto the streets.*"
—Vijay Prashad, author of *Darker Nations: A People's History of the Third World*

Anarchist Pedagogies: Collective Actions, Theories, and Critical Reflections on Education

Edited by Robert H. Haworth
with an Afterword by Allan Antliff

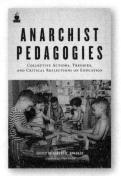

ISBN: 978-1-60486-484-7
$24.95   352 pages

Education is a challenging subject for anarchists. Many are critical about working within a state-run education system that is embedded in hierarchical, standardized, and authoritarian structures. Numerous individuals and collectives envision the creation of counterpublics or alternative educational sites as possible forms of resistance, while other anarchists see themselves as "saboteurs" within the public arena—believing that there is a need to contest dominant forms of power and educational practices from multiple fronts. Of course, if anarchists agree that there are no blueprints for education, the question remains, in what dynamic and creative ways can we construct nonhierarchical, anti-authoritarian, mutual, and voluntary educational spaces?

Contributors to this edited volume engage readers in important and challenging issues in the area of anarchism and education. From Francisco Ferrer's modern schools in Spain and the Work People's College in the United States, to contemporary actions in developing "free skools" in the U.K. and Canada, to direct-action education such as learning to work as a "street medic" in the protests against neoliberalism, the contributors illustrate the importance of developing complex connections between educational theories and collective actions. Anarchists, activists, and critical educators should take these educational experiences seriously as they offer invaluable examples for potential teaching and learning environments outside of authoritarian and capitalist structures. Major themes in the volume include: learning from historical anarchist experiments in education, ways that contemporary anarchists create dynamic and situated learning spaces, and finally, critically reflecting on theoretical frameworks and educational practices. Contributors include: David Gabbard, Jeffery Shantz, Isabelle Fremeaux & John Jordan, Abraham P. DeLeon, Elsa Noterman, Andre Pusey, Matthew Weinstein, Alex Khasnabish, and many others.